Contents

Introduction to Marketing Magic 4

   Understanding the Essence of Marketing 4

   The Magic of Building Strong Brands 6

   How Marketing Can Transform Your Business 10

Laying the Foundation 13

   Defining Your Unique Value Proposition (UVP) 13

   Identifying Your Target Audience and Buyer Personas 17

   Setting S.M.A.R.T. Marketing Goals 20

Crafting Enchanting Content 24

   The Art of Compelling Storytelling 24

   Creating Captivating Blog Posts and Articles 27

   Unleashing the Power of Visuals: Graphics and Infographics 30

Spellbinding Social Media Strategies 33

   Maximizing Impact on Social Media Platforms 33

   Building an Engaged Community of Followers 36

   The Magic of Social Media Advertising and Influencer Marketing 38

Casting SEO Spells for Visibility 41

   Unveiling the Secrets of Search Engine Optimization (SEO) 41

   Keyword Magic: How to Find and Use the Right Keywords 45

   Enchanting Your Content for Better Search Rankings 48

Potent Email Marketing Magic 53

   Building and Growing an Enchanting Email List 53

   Crafting Enthralling Email Campaign 57

   Nurturing Customer Relationships with Email Automation 61

Conjuring Conversion Magic 66

   Understanding the Customer Journey 66

   Enchanting Landing Pages for Higher Conversions 69

   A/B Testing and Optimization Spells 72

Harnessing the Power of Analytics 76

   Metrics That Matter: Measuring Marketing Success 76

   Interpreting Data for Growth Insights 79

   Data-Driven Decision Making: The Path to Marketing Mastery 83

Albanidis Dim. Konstantinos – Free Spirits Web Services

Embracing Influencer Alchemy 87

   Collaborating with Influencers: Finding the Right Fit 87

   Enchanting Partnerships for Mutual Benefit 89

   Measuring the Impact of Influencer Marketing 92

Putting It All Together: Crafting Your Marketing Strategy 96

   Creating an Integrated Marketing Plan 96

   Allocating Budgets for Maximum Impact 99

   Marketing Magic in Action: Real-Life Case Studies 102

Conclusion: Becoming a Marketing Sorcerer 106

   Embracing a Growth Mindset in Marketing 106

   Cultivating Continuous Learning and Adaptation 108

   Unleashing Your Full Marketing Potential 111

To my dearest wife, Iva Besheva,

I dedicate this book to you, my anchor, my rock, and my forever source of inspiration. Throughout this exhilarating marketing journey, you have been by my side, supporting and encouraging me every step of the way. You have been my guiding light, showing me unwavering love and offering a gentle push when doubt crept in.

Our children, Alex and Asia, are the cherry on top of this marvelous journey. Seeing their innocent smiles and feeling their endless love reminds me why I embarked on this marketing adventure in the first place.

To my beloved wife and cherished children, thank you for being my constant source of inspiration, strength, and love. This book is a small token of my gratitude and a reminder that you are the reason behind my triumphs. As our journey continues, I promise to hold your support and love close to my heart, never allowing them to wither.

With all my love and gratitude

Albanidis Dim. Konstantinos

Introduction to Marketing Magic

Understanding the Essence of Marketing

Imagine a world without marketing. No vibrant billboards flickering with enticing images, no catchy jingles echoing through your mind, and no carefully crafted advertisements vying for your attention. It would be a dreary existence, a society devoid of innovation and progress. Marketing, my dear reader, is the lifeblood that courses through the veins of our modern civilization.

At its core, marketing is the art of persuasive communication. It is the mechanism by which businesses captivate our attention, stimulate our desires, and ultimately convince us to exchange our hard-earned resources for their products and services. But it is so much more than that. It is the language of connection, the dance between supplier and consumer, the bridge that spans the gap between wants and needs. In the essence of marketing lies the power to shape not only the economy but also the very fabric of our society.

In today's hyper-connected world, the significance of marketing cannot be understated. It is the driving force behind the success or failure of businesses, big and small. It is the key differentiator in a sea of competitors, the guiding compass for entrepreneurs seeking growth and prosperity. In every industry, marketing is the conduit through which ideas are transformed into tangible realities and dreams into unstoppable movements.

Yet, in this vast landscape of marketing possibilities, where countless strategies and techniques abound, how does one navigate the treacherous terrain? Fear not, for this journey will be our mutual exploration. Together, we shall uncover the secrets and unravel the enigma of effective marketing.

Let us begin by immersing ourselves in the world of marketing strategies and techniques. From the traditional to the cutting-edge, we shall explore the arsenal at our disposal, examining their efficacy and impact on businesses. Through the depths of market segmentation, the heights of brand storytelling, and the intricacies of digital marketing, we will weave a tapestry of knowledge to empower you with the tools necessary for success.

While theories and concepts provide a strong foundation, it is the application of knowledge that truly unveils the transformative power of marketing. Thus, we shall venture into the realm of real-world case studies. Together, we will journey through the annals of history, examining the triumphs and tribulations of businesses as they navigated the unpredictable tides of the market. We shall dissect the strategies behind iconic campaigns, unraveling their impact and shedding light on the alchemy of effective marketing.

Picture this: A small, unassuming coffee shop arises amidst the cacophony of caffeine peddlers in a bustling city. Its name is unheard of, its offerings as humble as can be. And yet, through the magic of marketing, it transforms into a cultural phenomenon. People flock from all corners of the globe to experience the ethereal allure that this seemingly ordinary coffee house possesses. This tale, my friend, shall be merely one of the many stories we shall traverse together, as we decipher the code to marketing success.

As we embark on this journey, I promise you one thing: simplicity and clarity. The realm of marketing, often shrouded in mystique and complexity, shall be demystified. I seek to distill the intricate into palatable tidbits of knowledge, allowing even the most uninitiated to grasp the true essence of marketing.

So, dear reader, are you ready to dive headfirst into the enchanting world of marketing? Are you prepared to learn the intricacies and mysteries that lie at the heart of successful businesses? If so, hold tight, for we are about to embark on a journey that will forever alter your perception of the world around you. Welcome to the captivating odyssey of "Understanding the Essence of Marketing."

The Magic of Building Strong Brands

Every successful business harbors a secret ingredient that propels it to new heights – a powerful, alluring brand. Behind the seemingly effortless success of beloved companies lies a carefully crafted brand identity that captivates customers, establishes emotional connections, and fosters unwavering loyalty. Welcome to the world of building strong brands, where the magic happens and dreams transform into reality.

In this chapter, we embark on an exciting journey to unravel the fundamental principles of brand building that drive long-term success in the diverse marketing landscape. Drawing from a wealth of practical strategies, inspiring case studies, and insights from industry experts, we unveil the transformative power that lies within the creation of a strong brand identity. Are you ready to step into a world where brands come alive and hearts are won?

In the vast ocean of brands competing for consumer attention, differentiation is the key that unlocks success. What sets apart a brand that flourishes from one that fades into oblivion? The answer lies in crafting a unique identity that resonates with target audiences. To achieve this, marketers must understand their customers' needs, aspirations, and pain points. By conducting comprehensive market research and analysis, brands can uncover the gaps waiting to be filled and design offerings that cater specifically to those unmet desires.

 Case Study 1: Nike - Just Do It!

Nike, the iconic sportswear giant, recognized the need to differentiate itself in a crowded athletic apparel market. By studying its target audience – athletes and fitness enthusiasts – Nike tapped into the universal human desire for achievement. With the simple yet powerful slogan "Just Do It!" and a captivating brand narrative that resonated with determination and personal triumph, Nike differentiated itself from the competition, becoming a symbol of aspiration and success.

 Take Action: Conduct a thorough analysis of your target audience's needs, desires, and existing gaps in the market. Identify the unique qualities that set your brand apart and use them as the foundation for your brand story.

☀ Remember! Creating Lasting Connections

In a world driven by emotions, brands that elicit powerful feelings secure a place in the hearts and minds of consumers. Emotional resonance not only captures attention but also forges deep connections that endure.

By investing in powerful storytelling and evoking emotions aligned with their brand values, marketers can transform products and services into vehicles for deeply personal experiences.

Case Study 2: Coca-Cola - The Happiness Factory

Coca-Cola, a household name, has built an empire by creating moments of happiness. Through captivating advertisements, Coca-Cola transports viewers into a whimsical world filled with joy, togetherness, and unforgettable memories. By tapping into the universal emotion of happiness, Coca-Cola has consistently fostered emotional connections, transcending the boundaries of space and time.

Take Action: Define the emotions you want your brand to evoke and craft compelling stories that resonate with your target audience. Incorporate these narratives into your marketing campaigns, weaving an emotional connection between your brand and your customers.

Remember: Customer Loyalty - Nurturing Advocates for Life

The true measure of a strong brand lies not only in capturing customers but also in inspiring loyalty that transcends transactional relationships. Building customer loyalty requires an unwavering commitment to delivering exceptional experiences that consistently exceed expectations. By ensuring consistent quality, fostering authentic engagement, and actively listening to customer feedback, brands can cultivate a community of devoted brand advocates who willingly champion their products or services.

Case Study 3: Apple - Cultivating Devotion

Apple, the tech giant, has mastered the art of nurturing customer loyalty. With an unwavering focus on innovation, intuitive design, and seamless user experience, Apple's products create an emotional bond with their users. This loyalty is further reinforced by Apple's commitment to fostering an inclusive and passionate community, where customers become part of a larger brand family.

 Take Action: Invest in building long-term relationships with your customers by going above and beyond their expectations. Constantly seek feedback, create personalized experiences, and establish channels for open dialogue to foster deep connections and loyalty.

Empowering Brands and Marketers to Create Magic

As we conclude this chapter on the magic of building strong brands, we hope to have ignited your imagination and sparked a fire within, propelling you to take action and harness the transformative power of brand building. With the fundamental principles of brand differentiation, emotional resonance, and customer loyalty embedded in your marketing efforts, you can create a brand story that captivates and compels, turning customers into devoted brand advocates.

The magic of building strong brands lies not in mythical spells but in strategic planning, continuous innovation, and a deep understanding of your audience's desires. So, embark on this enchanting journey with your imagination as your guide. Unleash the transformative power within your brand and watch as it takes flight, leaving an indelible mark on the marketing world. Brace yourself, for you are about to discover the true magic of brand building.

How Marketing Can Transform Your Business

Marketing is not just about selling products or services; it is about creating an experience that captivates customers and establishes a strong bond with your brand. In today's rapidly changing business landscape, a comprehensive marketing strategy has the power to transform even the most stagnant businesses into thriving enterprises. This chapter explores the fundamental concepts of marketing and its role in driving business growth. We will delve into real-life examples and case studies that demonstrate how strategic marketing initiatives have successfully transformed businesses of various sizes and industries. Additionally, we will explore different marketing strategies, including digital marketing, branding, market research, and customer segmentation, and discuss the potential challenges and risks involved in implementing these strategies, along with effective solutions. By the end of this chapter, you will be armed with practical tips, actionable advice, and compelling storytelling techniques that will inspire you to harness the power of marketing for your own business success.

Marketing is not limited to advertising or promotions; it encompasses a wide range of activities aimed at understanding and satisfying customer needs profitably. It involves creating a comprehensive strategy to identify target markets, develop compelling products or services, communicate their value to customers, and build strong relationships to drive customer loyalty and advocacy.

Marketing is the catalyst for business growth. By understanding customer wants and needs and aligning them with the organization's core competencies, marketing drives revenue growth, increases market share, enhances brand awareness, and builds a loyal customer base.

 Case Studies:

Digital Marketing Transformation: How Airbnb Disrupted the Hospitality Industry:

Airbnb's pioneering digital marketing strategy revolutionized the hospitality industry. By leveraging the power of user-generated content, social media, and influencer marketing, Airbnb transformed from a small startup to a global behemoth. Through its unique storytelling approach and personalized experiences, they were able to connect with customers on a much deeper level, resulting in exponential growth and industry domination.

The Power of Branding: Coca-Cola's Enduring Legacy:

Coca-Cola's success lies not only in its iconic beverage but also in its ability to create a globally recognized brand. By consistently delivering an emotional experience, Coca-Cola has built a brand that transcends borders, cultures, and generations. Through clever marketing campaigns and brand extensions, Coca-Cola has maintained its dominance in the beverage space and continues to evolve to capture new markets and consumer segments.

 Marketing Strategies:

Market research is the backbone of successful marketing. Through an in-depth understanding of customer preferences, needs, and trends, organizations can develop products or services that truly resonate with their target market. In this section, we will explore how market research can help identify market gaps, consumer insights, and new opportunities, and allow for data-driven decision-making.

One size does not fit all, and customer segmentation enables businesses to deliver personalized experiences. We will dive into the importance of understanding different customer segments, their distinct needs and aspirations, and how tailoring marketing efforts to each segment can drive higher conversion rates, customer satisfaction, and long-term loyalty.

Implementing marketing strategies within limited resources can be a daunting challenge. We will discuss practical tips and cost-effective techniques, such as leveraging social media, utilizing content marketing, and harnessing the power of user-generated content, to make the most of your marketing budget.

In today's hypercompetitive marketplace, businesses face immense competition for customer attention. We will explore strategies for differentiation, value proposition communication, and cultivating a strong brand identity to ensure your business cuts through the noise and remains top of mind for your target audience.

 Conclusion:

Marketing is not an optional add-on; it is the lifeblood of business success. By effectively implementing marketing strategies tailored to your business and target audience, you can transform your organization from a struggling entity to a flourishing enterprise. In this chapter, we discussed the essence of marketing, examined real-life case studies, explored different marketing strategies, and provided solutions for common challenges. Armed with this knowledge and practical advice, you are now equipped to unleash the power of marketing and take your business to new heights. As you embark on this journey, remember that marketing is not just about selling; it is about creating a memorable brand experience that resonates with your customers, builds loyalty, and ultimately transforms your business.

Laying the Foundation

Defining Your Unique Value Proposition (UVP)

In a highly competitive market, businesses need to find ways to differentiate themselves and establish a strong brand identity. One of the most powerful tools in achieving this is a well-defined Unique Value Proposition (UVP). A UVP is a concise statement that communicates the unique benefits or value that a business offers to its customers, setting it apart from competitors. In this section, we will explore the importance of a UVP for businesses and guide you through the process of identifying and crafting a compelling UVP that resonates with your target customers.

A UVP is essential for businesses for several reasons. Firstly, it helps to communicate what sets your business apart from competitors in a concise and compelling manner. In a crowded marketplace, customers are often overwhelmed with choices. A strong UVP grabs their attention and highlights the specific benefits they can expect from doing business with you.

Secondly, a well-crafted UVP helps to establish a unique brand identity. It defines what your business stands for and what it promises to deliver to customers, creating a clear and consistent message that resonates with your target audience. By connecting with customers on an emotional and rational level, a UVP can foster loyalty and long-term relationships.

To identify a compelling UVP, start with a thorough understanding of your target market. Research your customers' needs, desires, pain points, and preferences. Consider what they value most and what problems they need solutions for. This information will be the foundation upon which you build your UVP. Here are the steps to follow:

1. Identify your target customers: Clearly define your target market and segment it based on demographics, psychographics, and behavior patterns.

2. Analyze competitors: Understand what your competitors are offering and how they position themselves in the market. Identify any gaps or opportunities where you can differentiate your business.

3. Determine your unique selling points: Identify the specific features, benefits, or qualities that make your business stand out. These can include factors such as superior quality, a comprehensive range of products or services, exceptional customer service, innovative technology, or a better price-value proposition.

4. Understand customer needs and desires: Study your target customers' needs, desires, and pain points. Look for opportunities to align your unique selling points with these customer needs to create a compelling value proposition.

 Take action: Crafting a compelling UVP:

Once you have identified your unique selling points and gained insights into your target customers' needs, it's time to craft a compelling UVP. Here are the steps:

1. Be concise: Your UVP should be a short, clear, and memorable statement that captures the essence of what your business offers. Keep it focused on the most compelling benefits and avoid jargon or complex language.

2. Highlight the benefits: Clearly communicate the unique benefits customers will experience by choosing your product or service. Explain why it is better than alternatives and how it addresses their specific pain points or desires.

3. Use persuasive language: Use powerful and persuasive language that appeals to your target audience's emotions and intellect. Choose words that create an emotional connection and convince customers that your business is the best choice.

4. Be specific and measurable: Whenever possible, include specific details that quantify the benefits your business offers. This could be in terms of cost savings, time saved, or tangible outcomes. Specificity helps to build credibility and trust.

 Remember: Illustrating the effectiveness of a well-defined UVP:

 Case Study 1: Apple - "Think Different"

Apple's UVP of "Think Different" in the late 1990s positioned the company as an innovative and rebellious brand, challenging the status quo. By emphasizing creativity, individuality, and a break from tradition, it appealed to customers who sought a unique computing experience. This UVP played a crucial role in Apple's successful rebranding and eventual dominance in the technology market.

Case Study 2: Tom's Shoes - "One for One"

Tom's Shoes introduced a UVP of "One for One," which emphasized their commitment to giving a pair of shoes to a person in need for every pair purchased. This UVP appealed to socially conscious consumers, who were willing to pay a premium for a product that made a positive impact on society. The UVP not only set Tom's Shoes apart from competitors but also created a powerful brand narrative.

Remember: Expert advice and best practices:

- Continuously evaluate and refine your UVP to stay relevant in a rapidly evolving market. Monitor market trends, customer feedback, and competitor activities to stay ahead.

- Focus on your target customers' needs and desires rather than trying to be everything to everyone. A narrow and targeted UVP is often more effective than a generic one.

- Be authentic and genuine in your UVP. Customers can quickly see through marketing gimmicks, so ensure your UVP aligns with your business's actual capabilities and values.

- Test your UVP with your target audience through surveys, focus groups, or A/B testing to gauge its effectiveness and refine it further.

In conclusion, a well-defined UVP is a vital component of any successful marketing strategy. It helps businesses differentiate themselves in a competitive market and creates a strong brand identity. By following the steps outlined in this section and drawing inspiration from relevant case studies, readers can create their own compelling UVPs that resonate with their target customers, ultimately driving business growth and success.

Identifying Your Target Audience and Buyer Personas

In the ever-evolving world of marketing, understanding your target audience is crucial for crafting effective strategies that resonate with potential customers. By identifying and defining your target audience, you can tailor your marketing messages and tactics specifically to the people who are most likely to be interested in your product or service. One effective way to accomplish this is by creating buyer personas, detailed representations of your ideal customers that encompass various traits and characteristics.

 The Importance of Understanding Your Target Audience

Understanding your target audience provides a strong foundation for your marketing efforts. It allows you to refine your messaging, select appropriate marketing channels, and create campaigns that resonate with your intended viewers. By clearly defining your target audience, you can avoid wasting resources on marketing to individuals who are unlikely to be interested in your product or service.

Take action: Step-by-Step Guidance Identifying and Defining Your Target Audience

1. Conduct Market Research: Start by conducting market research to gather demographic information about your potential customers. This could include age, gender, location, income level, education level, and occupation. By analyzing this data, you can identify patterns and trends that will help shape your target audience profile.

2. Analyze Consumer Preferences: Understanding consumer preferences is essential for effectively marketing your product or service.

Conduct surveys, and interviews, or analyze existing customer data to gain insights into consumer behavior, needs, and desires. Consider aspects such as their motivations, pain points, and purchase decision-making process.

3. Analyze Purchase Behavior: Study the buying behavior of your existing customers. Evaluate the channels they use for research, the factors that influence their purchasing decisions, and the triggers that lead them to convert. This analysis will help you understand where and how to position your marketing messages effectively.

4. Create a Target Audience Profile: Combine the data from your research and analysis to create a detailed profile of your target audience. Define their demographics, psychographics, and behaviors. This profile will serve as a reference point for crafting marketing messages that resonate with your ideal customer.

 The Significance of Buyer Personas

Once you have a clear understanding of your target audience, the next step is to create buyer personas. These fictional representations of your ideal customers provide a deeper understanding of their needs, motivations, goals, and challenges. Buyer personas go beyond basic demographic information and give you qualitative insights that help you tailor your marketing efforts more effectively.

 Tailoring Marketing Messages and Tactics

Buyer personas are especially valuable when it comes to crafting marketing messages and tactics that speak directly to your target audience. By aligning your messaging with their pain points, aspirations, and preferences, you can create personalized content that resonates with them on a deeper level. Whether it's through personalized emails, targeted social media campaigns, or customized website content, buyer personas enable you to deliver marketing materials that grab attention and drive engagement.

Practical Examples and Case Studies

To illustrate the benefits of understanding your target audience and creating buyer personas, let's explore a couple of practical examples. Suppose you are marketing a new line of athletic shoes designed for marathon runners. By conducting market research, you discover that the majority of marathon runners are between the ages of 25 and 45, have higher incomes, and reside in urban areas. Their pain points include injury prevention and maximizing performance.

Using this information, you can create a buyer persona named "Marathon Mike," a 35-year-old urban professional who actively participates in marathons. You can tailor your marketing campaign to highlight the shoes' features that address injury prevention and enhance performance, which would resonate with people like Marathon Mike. By incorporating Marathon Mike's persona into your marketing strategy, you can develop content, ad placements, and messaging that specifically target individuals who fit this profile.

Remember: Actionable Tips and Insights

To help readers apply these concepts to their own marketing campaigns, here are some actionable tips and insights:

1. Dive deep into market research and analytics to extract valuable insights about your target audience.

2. Engage with your existing customers to understand their preferences and pain points better.

3. Use surveys, interviews, or social listening tools to gather qualitative data that complements your quantitative research.

4. Continuously monitor market trends and adjust your target audience profile and buyer personas accordingly.

5. Don't be afraid to refine your target audience and buyer personas as you gather more data and insights.

6. Regularly revisit your marketing strategy and tactics to ensure they align with your target audience and buyer personas.

By understanding your target audience and creating buyer personas, you can position your marketing messages and tactics with precision. This approach enables you to optimize your marketing efforts, maximize engagement, and increase conversion rates. So, invest the time and resources into identifying your target audience and creating buyer personas - your marketing campaigns will thank you.

Setting S.M.A.R.T. Marketing Goals

In the world of marketing, setting goals is crucial for success. However, many marketers often struggle with creating goals that are specific, measurable, attainable, relevant, and time-bound – a concept commonly referred to as S.M.A.R.T. goals. In this section, we will explore the importance of S.M.A.R.T. goals in the marketing industry, provide step-by-step instructions on how to create them, and discuss the benefits they bring to marketing campaigns.

Why S.M.A.R.T. Goals are Important in Marketing:

S.M.A.R.T. goals are essential for marketers because they provide a clear roadmap to success. They outline specific targets, help measure progress, and ensure that marketing efforts are aligned with the overall business objectives. Without well-defined goals, campaigns can lack focus, waste resources, and fail to achieve desired outcomes. By implementing S.M.A.R.T. goals, marketers can enhance their productivity, track their success, and continuously improve their strategies.

✳ Take action: Creating S.M.A.R.T. Marketing Goals

Step 1: Be specific

The first step in creating S.M.A.R.T. marketing goals is to make them specific. This means defining the goal in precise terms, leaving no room for ambiguity. For example, instead of saying "increase sales," a specific S.M.A.R.T. goal would be "increase online sales by 15% in the next quarter." This ensures that everyone involved understands the objective and can work towards achieving it.

Step 2: Make it measurable

A measurable goal allows marketers to track progress and determine success. To ensure measurability, attach a quantifiable metric to your goal. For instance, in the above example, you can measure progress by tracking the percentage increase in online sales. This measurement provides valuable insights and enables marketers to assess the effectiveness of their strategies.

Step 3: Set attainable goals

Setting attainable goals is crucial to maintain motivation and prevent disappointment. While it is essential to stretch the limits, goals that are too far out of reach may demoralize the team. Consider factors such as available resources, budget, and time constraints when setting goals. For example, increasing online sales by 500% in a month may be unrealistic, while aiming for a 15% increase could be more feasible.

Step 4: Ensure relevance

Relevance is crucial to align marketing goals with business objectives. Each goal should contribute directly to the overall success of the organization. For instance, if the business objective is to expand into a new market, a relevant marketing goal might be to increase brand awareness in that specific market segment. By ensuring relevance, marketers can focus efforts on activities that truly impact the bottom line.

Step 5: Make it time-bound

Setting a timeframe for achieving goals provides a sense of urgency and helps measure progress effectively. Without a deadline, goals may remain as aspirations rather than actionable plans. For example, setting a goal to increase brand engagement on social media by 25% within three months provides a clear time-bound objective that can be measured and tracked.

 Benefits of S.M.A.R.T. Marketing Goals:

Setting S.M.A.R.T. marketing goals offers numerous benefits to marketers and their campaigns. Firstly, they provide a focal point, enabling marketers to prioritize efforts and allocate resources effectively. This focus also improves decision-making, as marketers can assess which strategies contribute directly to goal achievement. Secondly, S.M.A.R.T. goals allow for clear measurement of results. They enable marketers to track progress, evaluate the effectiveness of their campaigns, and make data-driven adjustments. Thirdly, S.M.A.R.T. goals enhance accountability. Teams are more likely to take ownership of their tasks when goals are clearly defined and time-bound, leading to increased efficiency and productivity.

Common Challenges and Practical Tips:

Implementing S.M.A.R.T. goals may present challenges for marketers. One common challenge is the inability to accurately measure progress due to insufficient data or unreliable tracking systems. To overcome this, invest in analytics tools and ensure data collection methods are robust. Another challenge is setting unrealistic goals. To avoid this, conduct thorough research, evaluate past performance, and involve relevant stakeholders in goal setting. Lastly, limited resources can hinder goal achievement. In these cases, marketers should prioritize goals and identify the most impactful activities that can be executed within the available resources.

Conclusion:

S.M.A.R.T. goals are a fundamental aspect of effective marketing strategies. By following the step-by-step process outlined in this section, marketers can create goals that are specific, measurable, attainable, relevant, and time-bound. These goals provide enhanced focus, allow for measurable results, and increase accountability. By understanding the importance, benefits, and potential pitfalls of S.M.A.R.T. goal setting, marketers can chart a course for success and drive their marketing efforts toward achieving tangible and meaningful outcomes.

Crafting Enchanting Content

The Art of Compelling Storytelling

In the fast-paced world of marketing, where attention spans are fleeting and consumers are bombarded with endless messages, the need to captivate and engage has never been more crucial. In this chapter, we will explore the art of compelling storytelling and its immense importance in marketing. Through practical tips, best practices, and real-life examples, we will uncover the power of storytelling to elevate brand awareness, forge lasting connections with customers, and ultimately drive business success.

The Power of Storytelling in Marketing

Storytelling taps into the core of what it means to be human – our innate desire for connection and understanding. When done well, it transcends the noise of traditional marketing techniques, allowing brands to establish genuine emotional connections with their audience. As research has shown, our brains are hardwired to respond to narratives, making storytelling a powerful tool in capturing attention and fostering brand loyalty.

 Practical Tips for Effective Storytelling

1. Create relatable characters: The key to a compelling story lies in relatable characters that resonate with your target audience. Crafting personas that embody the values, aspirations, and challenges of your ideal customers will facilitate emotional connections and engagement. Consider success stories of real people who have interacted with your brand and use their experiences as the foundation for your narrative.

2. Utilize emotional appeals: Emotions are the secret ingredient that can transform a story from forgettable to unforgettable. Incorporate feelings such as joy, empathy, nostalgia, or even a touch of humor into your storytelling. By triggering an emotional response, your brand becomes personally relevant to your audience, further strengthening the bond between them and your business.

3. Structure narratives to keep audiences engaged: Borrow techniques from the world of fiction to structure your marketing narratives effectively. Begin with a powerful hook to grab attention, develop a compelling conflict or challenge, and conclude with a resolution that showcases the impact your brand has made. This storytelling structure creates a sense of anticipation and keeps your audience engaged until the very end.

 Real-Life Examples

Dove's "Real Beauty" campaign is legendary for its impactful storytelling. By showcasing real women with diverse body types and challenging the beauty industry's narrow standards, Dove tapped into a universal desire for acceptance and empowerment. The campaign's emotional appeal helped Dove not only gain immense brand loyalty but also sparked a global conversation on beauty standards.

Nike's "Just Do It" slogan has become synonymous with overcoming adversity, thanks to its use of compelling narratives. By featuring athletes who have triumphed over setbacks and challenges, Nike conveys a powerful message of resilience and determination. Their storytelling strategy has transformed their brand into a symbol of aspiration and achievement.

 Expert Insights and Advice

Research has consistently shown that storytelling activates multiple areas of the brain, making it more memorable than dry, fact-based marketing. Incorporating storytelling into your marketing strategy can differentiate your brand from competitors and leave a lasting impression on your audience.

To effectively incorporate storytelling, it is crucial to truly understand your target audience, their desires, and the challenges they face. Tailor your narratives to align with their values and aspirations, demonstrating how your brand can meet their needs and aspirations.

 Conclusion

Incorporating storytelling into your marketing strategy is a powerful tool that brings your brand to life, resonates with customers, and differentiates you from competitors. Through relatable characters, emotional appeals, and structured narratives, you can create experiences that captivate and engage your audience on a deeper level. By embracing the art of compelling storytelling, you can elevate your marketing efforts, build brand awareness, and forge enduring relationships with your customers.

Creating Captivating Blog Posts and Articles

In today's digital age, attention is a scarce resource. With countless blog posts and articles vying for readers' attention, how can you ensure that your content stands out from the crowd? In this section, we will explore practical tips and strategies for crafting compelling blog posts and articles that grab readers' attention and keep them engaged.

1. Unique and Valuable Content: The foundation of captivation lies in the creation of unique and valuable content. Your audience is constantly seeking new insights and experiences. To captivate them, offer something they can't find elsewhere. Whether it's a fresh perspective, groundbreaking research, or practical solutions to their problems, always strive to deliver content that offers genuine value.

Example: The blog post "10 Science-Backed Habits for a Productive Morning Routine" by productivity guru Jane Smith successfully went viral. By providing scientifically proven strategies to enhance productivity, Smith crafted a unique and valuable resource that resonated with readers.

2. The Power of Storytelling: We are wired to connect emotionally with stories. Incorporating storytelling techniques into your blog posts and articles can take your readers on a captivating journey. Use anecdotes, personal experiences, and relatable narratives to engage and resonate with your audience on a deeper level.

Example: The article "From Homelessness to Forbes: My Journey of Triumph" by entrepreneur John Doe captured readers' hearts by weaving a powerful story of overcoming adversity. Through his personal journey, Doe inspired and motivated readers to pursue their dreams.

👉 3. Visuals for Enhanced Reader Experience: Incorporating visuals into your content can greatly enhance the reader experience. Visuals not only capture attention but also help convey information more effectively. Use captivating images, infographics, videos, and charts to break up text and make your content more engaging and shareable.

Example: The blog post "Top 10 Travel Destinations of 2022: A Photographic Journey" by travel photographer Sarah Johnson combined stunning visuals with travel recommendations. The immersive experience created by the visuals kept readers captivated and fueled their desire to explore new destinations.

👉 4. Crafting Effective Headlines: The headline is your hook, the first chance to capture the reader's attention. Craft attention-grabbing headlines that spark curiosity, promise value and evoke emotion. Use power words, numbers, and questions to pique readers' interest and make them click through to your content.

Example: The headline "7 Secrets to Unleash Your Inner Creativity" by creativity coach Emily Thompson captured readers' attention by promising to reveal valuable insights they could apply immediately.

👉 5. Structuring Content for Readability: Captivating content needs to be easily digestible. Structure your blog posts and articles with subheadings, bullet points, and clear paragraphs. Break up the text into bite-sized chunks that allow readers to skim and quickly grasp the main points. Use concise and straightforward language, eliminating jargon that might deter readers.

6. Persuasive Language to Inspire Action: To truly captivate your readers, your content should inspire action. Utilize persuasive language to create a sense of urgency, foster engagement, and encourage readers to implement your recommendations. Use active verbs, create a compelling call-to-action, and invoke emotions that push readers to take the desired action.

Actionable Steps and Exercises:

1. Identify a popular blog post or article in your niche that went viral. Analyze what made it captivating and appealing to readers.

2. Choose a personal anecdote or story that aligns with your content's main message. Incorporate this storytelling technique into your next blog post or article.

3. Create a visual element (image, infographic, or video) to accompany your next piece of content. Experiment with different visual formats to find the ones that best enhance your message.

4. Brainstorm attention-grabbing headlines for your upcoming articles. Utilize power words, numbers, and questions to create intrigue and evoke curiosity.

5. Review your current content structure. Identify areas where you can break up text into smaller, scannable chunks and utilize subheadings and bullet points.

6. Practice incorporating persuasive language into your writing. Develop a call-to-action that inspires action and encourages readers to engage with your content.

By implementing these techniques and strategies, you will be equipped to create captivating blog posts and articles that grab readers' attention, keep them engaged and inspire action. Remember that captivating content is not just about attracting readers; it is about creating valuable experiences that resonate and leave a lasting impact.

Unleashing the Power of Visuals: Graphics and Infographics

In today's fast-paced digital landscape, marketers are constantly seeking innovative ways to capture the attention of their target audiences. As attention spans shrink, the power of visual content has become more crucial than ever before. Graphics and infographics, in particular, have emerged as game-changers in marketing strategies, enabling businesses to effectively convey complex messages and connect with their audience in a compelling and memorable manner. In this section, we will explore the importance of visual content in marketing strategies and provide practical tips and effective techniques for creating impactful graphics and infographics.

Visual content has long been recognized as a powerful tool to engage and communicate messages. Research indicates that visuals are processed by the human brain 60,000 times faster than text, making them the ideal medium to capture attention in our increasingly visually-driven society. Whether it's social media posts, blog articles, or website landing pages, incorporating visually appealing graphics and infographics within marketing materials can significantly enhance the effectiveness of communication.

One key benefit of utilizing graphics and infographics is their ability to simplify complex information. Instead of bombarding your audience with lengthy, text-heavy content, you can present data and concepts in a visually appealing and easy-to-understand manner. Case studies have shown that including infographics in your marketing campaigns can increase website traffic by a staggering 12%, as it allows your audience to quickly grasp the essence of your message.

To create impactful graphics and infographics, it's essential to prioritize simplicity and clarity. Keep in mind that your audience is often bombarded with information overload, so focus on delivering a concise and visually appealing message. Use eye-catching colors, bold typography, and relevant imagery to grab attention and maintain interest. Experiment with different designs and layouts to find the best fit for your brand and target audience. Don't be afraid to be creative and think outside the box.

Industry leaders have successfully incorporated visual content into their marketing strategies, resulting in significant growth and brand recognition. Take, for example, Dollar Shave Club's humorous and visually engaging explainer video that launched their brand into stardom. The video quickly went viral, generating millions of views and subscribers. By incorporating humor, relatable characters, and a clear value proposition, Dollar Shave Club effectively captured their audience's attention, conveying their message in an unforgettable way.

Visuals also play a crucial role in enhancing brand identity. Consistency in design elements, such as color schemes, typography, and visual style, can create a strong visual brand that resonates with your audience. When crafting visuals, it's important to align them with your brand's personality and values, enabling your audience to associate those visuals directly with your brand. This can lead to increased brand recognition, recall, and ultimately, customer loyalty.

However, while graphics and infographics offer immense potential, there are challenges to navigate. One such challenge is the ever-changing nature of design trends and consumer preferences. To remain relevant, it's essential to stay updated on the latest design aesthetics and incorporate them into your visuals. Conduct thorough research, keep an eye on design blogs and social media platforms, and analyze successful campaigns to identify emerging trends and adapt accordingly.

Additionally, it's crucial to strike the right balance between aesthetics and comprehensibility. While visually stunning graphics and infographics can be captivating, they must effectively convey the intended message without overwhelming the viewer. Always test your visuals with your target audience to ensure clarity and avoid any confusion in the communication process.

In conclusion, visuals have become an indispensable part of any successful marketing strategy. Graphics and infographics offer a unique opportunity to engage your audience, simplify complex information, enhance brand identity, attract customers, and drive engagement. By paying attention to design trends, staying true to your brand's identity, and maintaining clarity in your visuals, you can unleash the power of visual storytelling to captivate your audience and achieve marketing success.

Spellbinding Social Media Strategies

Maximizing Impact on Social Media Platforms

In an era where social media has become an integral part of our everyday lives, businesses cannot afford to overlook the potential it holds for marketing and engaging with their audience. To effectively harness the power of these platforms, strategies and tactics need to be employed to ensure businesses achieve their marketing goals and create a strong online presence. In this section, we will explore proven strategies and techniques that successful brands and individuals have employed to maximize their impact on social media platforms.

Content Optimization: The key to engaging with an audience on social media lies in creating compelling and optimized content. Businesses must understand their target audience, their interests, and the type of content that resonates with them. Conducting thorough research on trending topics and keywords can guide businesses in creating content that is not only engaging but also optimized for search engine discoverability.

Case Study: Tasty, a popular food network, has revolutionized content optimization on social media platforms. Their bite-sized recipe videos are visually appealing, engaging, and optimized for maximum reach. By understanding their audience's preference for quick and easy recipes, Tasty has amassed millions of followers and secured their position as a go-to source for cooking inspiration.

Influencer Collaborations: Leveraging the power of influencers can significantly enhance a business's reach on social media. Partnering with influencers who align with a business's target audience allows for authentic and relatable content promotion. By tapping into an influencer's existing follower base, businesses can introduce their brand to a wider audience and potentially gain new customers.

Case Study: Gymshark, a fitness apparel brand, has effectively utilized influencer collaborations to enhance their reach on social media. By partnering with fitness enthusiasts and influencers to showcase their products in action, they have been able to tap into a dedicated community. The trust and credibility established through these collaborations have helped Gymshark build a strong online presence and become a market leader.

Leveraging Analytics for Targeted Campaigns: Utilizing social media analytics and insights allows businesses to better understand their audience's behavior and preferences. By analyzing metrics such as reach, engagement, and demographics, businesses can align their content strategies with their audience's interests, maximizing the impact of their campaigns.

 Case Study: Starbucks, a global coffee chain, has effectively utilized analytics to target campaigns on social media. By monitoring specific locations, demographics, and peak consumption times, Starbucks can tailor their social media campaigns to specific audiences. This targeted approach has resulted in increased engagement levels and higher conversion rates.

Practical Tips and Actionable Insights:

1. Encourage user-generated content by creating contests or campaigns that encourage followers to share their experiences with your brand. This not only boosts engagement but also provides businesses with a powerful form of social proof.

2. Actively engage with your audience by responding to comments, messages, and reviews. This fosters a sense of community and builds trust between the brand and its followers.

3. Experiment with new features and formats offered by social media platforms, such as live videos, stories, or polls. These features can help businesses present content in unique and engaging ways, further enhancing their reach.

4. Continuously track and analyze key performance indicators to measure the success of your social media efforts. This data-driven approach allows for optimization and further refinement of content strategies.

By implementing these strategies and tactics, businesses can effectively engage with their audience on social media platforms and maximize their impact. Case studies and examples from successful brands and individuals provide real-world inspiration and validation of these strategies. By leveraging content optimization, influencer collaborations, and analytics, businesses can amplify their reach, enhance their online presence, and achieve their marketing goals.

Building an Engaged Community of Followers

In today's digital age, marketers have recognized the immense value of building an engaged community of followers. A loyal and active following not only amplifies your marketing efforts but also serves as a powerful word-of-mouth marketing tool and a reliable source of feedback and insights. To cultivate a strong and engaged following, marketers must employ various strategies and tactics that revolve around understanding their target audience, creating meaningful and valuable content, and fostering two-way communication with their followers.

Understanding Your Target Audience: The first step in building an engaged community is to truly understand your target audience. Conduct thorough market research to gain insights into their needs, desires, pain points, and preferences. Dive deep into their demographics, psychographics, behaviors, and social media habits to develop a comprehensive understanding of who they are and what they value. By understanding your audience, you can tailor your content and messaging to resonate with them, thus increasing engagement and fostering a sense of community.

Creating Meaningful and Valuable Content: Content is king when it comes to building an engaged following. However, it's not just about creating any content - it's about crafting meaningful and valuable content that speaks to your audience's interests and challenges. Develop a content strategy that aligns with your brand's values and objectives, and consistently deliver high-quality content that educates, entertains, or inspires your followers. Whether it's informative blog posts, engaging videos, or captivating social media campaigns, your content should provide value and encourage active participation from your community.

Fostering Two-Way Communication: Building an engaged community relies heavily on fostering two-way communication with your followers. Gone are the days of one-sided conversations; today's consumers expect brands to listen and respond. Actively engage with your audience by replying to comments, direct messages, and social media mentions. Encourage feedback and reviews, and use them as opportunities to improve and show your community that their opinions matter. Create dedicated spaces, such as online forums or interactive live sessions, where your followers can connect with each other and share their experiences, thus fostering a sense of belonging and community.

Practical Tips and Techniques:

1. Personalize Your Communication: Address your followers by their names and acknowledge their contributions to build a genuine connection.

2. Be Consistent: Establish a regular content publishing schedule and stick to it. Consistency helps build trust and expectation amongst your followers.

3. Use Gamification: Incorporate elements of gamification, such as contests or challenges, to encourage active participation and create a sense of excitement within your community.

Case Studies and Real-World Examples:

1. Apple's "Today at Apple" Program: Apple created an in-store program that offers educational experiences to its customers. By fostering hands-on learning and community engagement, Apple has successfully built a community of loyal followers who see the brand as an enabler of creativity and growth.

2. Glossier's "Into the Gloss" Blog: Glossier, a beauty brand, strategically launched a blog called "Into the Gloss" that shares skincare and beauty secrets. By providing valuable content and encouraging discussions, the blog helped the brand connect with its followers on a deeper level, resulting in a dedicated community of beauty enthusiasts.

By following these strategies and implementing practical tips, marketers can inspire and equip themselves with the tools needed to cultivate a strong and engaged following for their marketing efforts. Remember, building a community takes time and consistent effort, but the rewards in terms of brand loyalty, advocacy, and valuable insights make it a worthwhile investment.

The Magic of Social Media Advertising and Influencer Marketing

In today's fast-paced digital landscape, social media advertising and influencer marketing have cast a spell on modern businesses, reshaping the way they connect with their target audience and build strong, authentic relationships. Gone are the days of traditional marketing channels reigning supreme; social media platforms have emerged as the stage upon which brands can captivate their audiences, enchanting them with compelling stories and establishing a loyal following.

The profound impact of social media advertising and influencer marketing lies in their ability to transcend the limitations of traditional advertising. Brands have uncovered the power of using social media platforms to directly engage with their audience, creating a two-way conversation rather than merely shouting from a distance. By harnessing the vast reach and targeting capabilities of platforms like Facebook, Instagram, and Twitter, brands can deliver highly tailored messages to precisely the audience they seek.

Case studies and success stories are a testament to the immense potential of this marketing approach. Take Nike, for instance, which collaborated with renowned athlete Serena Williams to promote their line of sports apparel. By leveraging Serena's influence and personal brand on Instagram, Nike was able to connect with female athletes on a deep level. The campaign generated buzz, driving significant engagement and sales. The magic lies in the genuine rapport and trust between the influencer and their audience, establishing a bond that traditional advertisements often struggle to achieve.

One of the key benefits of social media advertising and influencer marketing is the ability to organically integrate brands into the lives of consumers. They no longer feel bombarded with disruptive advertisements but rather engage with content that feels more like a friend's recommendation than a marketing ploy. The authenticity of these partnerships creates a seamless experience, providing value to consumers while achieving the brand's objectives.

However, as with any spell, challenges may arise when implementing social media advertising and influencer marketing campaigns. The first hurdle is finding the right influencer that aligns with your brand's values and target audience. With countless influencers in the digital realm, it is crucial to choose those whose personal brand and followers genuinely resonate with your brand's identity. Additionally, transparency is crucial in maintaining trust and credibility. Brands must be cautious to disclose any partnerships or sponsorships, ensuring consumers can distinguish between genuine endorsements and paid promotions.

To maximize the effectiveness of social media advertising and influencer marketing, businesses should focus on fostering authenticity and transparent partnerships. Consumers can quickly detect disingenuity, so it is crucial to align influencer collaborations and content creation with the brand's values. Encourage influencers to speak from their unique perspectives, giving them the freedom to showcase their genuine experiences and opinions. By creating a transparent and authentic connection with their target audience, brands can harness the magic of social media advertising and influencer marketing to drive conversions and build enduring relationships.

As you embark on your own marketing endeavors, remember the magic that social media advertising and influencer marketing can bring to your brand. Allow yourself to be enchanted by the endless possibilities these strategies offer. Embrace the power of social media to establish meaningful connections, and watch as the magic unfolds before your eyes.

Casting SEO Spells for Visibility

Unveiling the Secrets of Search Engine Optimization (SEO)

Search Engine Optimization (SEO) holds the key to successful digital marketing. As the digital landscape evolves and becomes increasingly competitive, understanding and mastering SEO techniques have become essential for businesses to gain online visibility and attract organic traffic. In this chapter, we will explore the ins and outs of SEO, including keyword research, on-page optimization, link building, and content strategy. We will discuss the importance of staying updated on search engine algorithms and highlight the potential results and pitfalls of implementing different SEO strategies.

 Keyword Research

Keywords are the foundation of SEO as they determine how search engines understand and rank your content. Conducting effective keyword research helps businesses identify the language and phrases their target audience uses when searching for products or services. Here are some essential tips and techniques for successful keyword research:

1. Begin with a brainstorming session: Start by jotting down words and phrases relevant to your business. Consider what your audience might search for and how your products or services address their needs.

2. Leverage keyword research tools: Utilize tools like Google Keyword Planner, SEMrush, or Moz Keyword Explorer to gain insights into search volume, competition, and related keywords. These tools can help you identify valuable keywords to target.

3. Understand user intent: Analyze the intention behind specific keywords and tailor your content accordingly. Keywords can be classified into informational (seeking knowledge), transactional (ready to make a purchase), or navigational (looking for a specific website).

On-Page Optimization

On-page optimization refers to the strategies employed within the webpage to improve its visibility and relevancy for search engines. Here are some key on-page optimization techniques:

1. Title tags and meta descriptions: Craft compelling and relevant title tags and meta descriptions that accurately describe the content of the webpage. These elements appear in search results, influencing click-through rates.

2. Optimize headers and content: Use descriptive H1, H2, and H3 tags to structure your content. Include relevant keywords naturally throughout the content to ensure search engine crawlers understand its relevance.

3. Improve site speed and mobile responsiveness: Optimize your website to provide fast loading times and ensure it is mobile-friendly. Google considers these factors when ranking websites, as they enhance the user experience.

 Link Building

Link building remains a fundamental aspect of SEO, as search engines view external links as indicators of a website's credibility and relevance. However, it is essential to implement link-building strategies carefully and ethically. Here are some best practices for link building:

1. High-quality backlinks: Focus on acquiring backlinks from reputable and authoritative websites. Relevance and quality matter more than quantity.

2. Guest blogging: Contribute valuable content to authoritative websites in your industry to secure contextual backlinks. Ensure the content is informative, engaging, and aligns with the host website's target audience.

3. Building internal links: Connect relevant pages within your website by incorporating internal links. This helps search engine crawlers navigate and understand your website's structure.

 Content Strategy

Content that provides value to users while targeting relevant keywords is the cornerstone of SEO success. Developing a comprehensive content strategy involves the following:

1. Creating in-depth and engaging content: Produce high-quality content that offers actionable insights, solves problems, and captivates your audience. Focus on creating long-form content that covers a topic comprehensively.

2. Incorporating rich media: Enhance your content by incorporating images, infographics, videos, and other visual elements. Rich media makes your content more engaging and shareable.

3. Repurposing content: Maximize the value of your content by repurposing it in various formats. For example, a blog post can be turned into a video, an infographic, or a podcast, extending its reach and appeal.

Keeping Pace with Algorithm Updates

Search engine algorithms are dynamic and continually evolving. Staying updated with these changes ensures your SEO strategies remain effective. Here are some ways to keep pace with algorithm updates:

1. Follow reputable SEO blogs and forums: Stay informed about the latest industry news, algorithm updates, and best practices through trustworthy sources like Search Engine Land, Moz, and Google Webmaster Central Blog.

2. Monitor website analytics: Regularly analyze your website's performance, rankings, and traffic trends. Identify any sudden drops or spikes that may indicate the impact of algorithm updates.

3. Continual learning and experimentation: SEO is a constantly evolving field. Stay curious, experiment with new techniques, and adapt your strategies as required.

 Conclusion:

Search Engine Optimization is a powerful marketing tool that enables businesses to increase their online visibility and attract qualified organic traffic. By conducting effective keyword research, optimizing on-page elements, building high-quality backlinks, and implementing a comprehensive content strategy, businesses can achieve sustained SEO success. However, it is crucial to stay updated with ever-evolving search engine algorithms to ensure the consistency and effectiveness of your SEO efforts. By following the proven strategies outlined in this chapter and consistently adapting to industry changes, businesses can unlock the true potential of SEO and drive their digital marketing initiatives to new heights.

Keyword Magic: How to Find and Use the Right Keywords

In today's digital era, effective keyword research is essential for successful marketing campaigns. By understanding how to find and use the right keywords, businesses can optimize their website content and drive organic traffic. This section will provide step-by-step guidance on conducting keyword research effectively, utilizing various tools and techniques.

Start with brainstorming: Begin by brainstorming a list of relevant words and phrases that potential customers may use to find products or services related to your business. Think about specific features, benefits, or problems that your offerings address.

Example: A clothing retailer may brainstorm keywords like "women's dresses," "summer fashion," or "affordable clothing."

Use keyword research tools: There are several tools available that provide valuable insights into keyword popularity and competition. Platforms like Google Trends, Google AdWords' Keyword Planner, and Moz's Keyword Explorer are excellent resources to determine search volume and discover related keywords.

Example: By using Google AdWords' Keyword Planner, the clothing retailer may find popular keywords such as "summer maxi dresses" or "affordable sundresses."

Analyze competition and search intent: Once you have a list of potential keywords, it's essential to evaluate the competition and understand the user's intent behind each keyword. Evaluate the top-ranking websites for each keyword to determine if you can compete with their content quality.

Example: The clothing retailer may find that "summer dresses under $50" has a relatively low competition level compared to "women's dresses," indicating a higher chance of ranking well.

Leverage long-tail keywords: Long-tail keywords are longer, more specific phrases that have lower competition but higher intent. These keywords attract users who are closer to making a purchase decision.

Example: Instead of targeting the highly competitive keyword "dresses," the clothing retailer could use a long-tail keyword like "summer maxi dresses for beach weddings," capturing a niche audience actively searching for a specific product.

Optimize website content: Incorporate the selected keywords strategically into your website content. Ensure they are included in the meta tags, headings, alt text for images, and naturally throughout the body of your content. However, avoid overstuffing keywords, as it can negatively impact user experience and search engine rankings.

Example: The clothing retailer can optimize their website content by writing a blog post titled "10 Trendy Summer Maxi Dresses for Beach Weddings," incorporating the long-tail keyword into the title, headings, and body of the content.

By selecting relevant keywords and incorporating them into your website content, you can improve search engine rankings and increase organic traffic. Properly optimized websites help search engines understand your content's relevance, making it more likely to appear in search results.

Real-world success stories illustrate the effectiveness of proper keyword usage. For instance, by implementing a targeted keyword strategy, a gourmet coffee company increased its organic traffic by 150% within three months. Another case study showcased a software business that achieved a 50% increase in conversion rates by optimizing landing pages with long-tail keywords.

In conclusion, keyword research is a vital component of digital marketing. By effectively identifying and utilizing the right keywords, businesses can enhance their website's visibility, attract targeted traffic, and ultimately drive successful marketing campaigns.

Enchanting Your Content for Better Search Rankings

When it comes to marketing, optimizing your content for search engines has become essential in today's digital landscape. With millions of websites vying for attention, ensuring your content ranks high in search engine result pages (SERPs) can make a significant difference in driving organic traffic to your website. This section will delve into the importance of content optimization for search engines, provide strategies and tips for improving search rankings, and shed light on the latest trends and best practices in the field.

1. Understanding the Importance of Content Optimization:

Effective content optimization helps search engines understand and categorize your website, enhancing its visibility to potential customers. By aligning your content with popular search queries, you increase the likelihood of appearing in relevant SERPs, driving qualified organic traffic to your site. This, in turn, can boost your brand's visibility, lead generation, and ultimately, business growth.

2. Conducting Keyword Research:

Keyword research forms the foundation of content optimization. Identify the specific words and phrases potential customers are likely to use when searching for products, information, or services related to your industry. Utilize keyword research tools like Google Keyword Planner, SEMrush, or Moz Keyword Explorer to uncover high-volume, low-competition keywords with strong relevance to your content. Aim for a mix of long-tail and short-tail keywords to capture different user search intents.

 3. On-Page Optimization Techniques:

Once you've identified your target keywords, it's crucial to optimize your content for them. Here are some key on-page optimization techniques to enhance search rankings:

a) Include target keywords strategically: Incorporate your target keywords naturally in key elements such as the title tag, meta description, headings, and throughout the content. However, avoid keyword stuffing, as it may harm your rankings.

b) Craft compelling meta descriptions: Write concise, engaging meta descriptions that accurately summarize your content. This helps search engines and users understand what to expect, increasing click-through rates from the SERPs.

c) Optimize headings and subheadings: Utilize HTML heading tags (H1, H2, H3, etc.) to structure your content. Incorporate variations of your target keywords in these headings to signal relevance to both readers and search engines.

✳ d) Optimize URL structure: Craft clean, descriptive, and keyword-rich URLs. Instead of using a generic URL like "www.example.com/blog/article-1234," opt for something like "www.example.com/blog/content-optimization-strategies."

✳ e) Optimize image attributes: Optimize alt text, file names, and captions for images on your website. This allows search engines to understand what the image represents, enhancing overall content relevance.

💡 4. The Role of Backlinks in SEO:

Backlinks play a crucial role in determining your website's credibility and authority in the eyes of search engines. A backlink is a link from another website to yours. Search engines interpret backlinks as endorsements, assuming that if other reputable websites link to your content, it must be valuable. Aim to foster high-quality, relevant backlinks by:

✳ a) Creating quality content: Craft informative, unique, and engaging content that provides value to your target audience. Quality content naturally attracts backlinks from authoritative sources.

✳ b) Conducting outreach: Proactively reach out to relevant websites in your industry, offering them your high-quality content for potential inclusion in their articles or resources.

 c) Guest blogging: Produce insightful guest posts for reputable websites in your industry, and include a well-placed link back to your content. This not only helps build backlinks but also introduces your brand to new audiences.

d) Engaging with influencers: Build relationships with influencers in your niche. Collaborating with them through interviews, expert opinions, or joint content creation can result in valuable backlinks and increased visibility.

5. Latest Trends and Best Practices:

To stay ahead in the constantly evolving world of content optimization, it's crucial to be aware of the latest trends and best practices. Here are a few key areas to focus on:

a) Mobile optimization: Ensure your website is responsive and mobile-friendly. With the rise of mobile internet usage, search engines prioritize mobile-optimized content.

b) Voice search optimization: As voice search continues to gain popularity, optimize your content to capture long-tail, conversational keywords that align with user voice queries.

c) User experience (UX): Optimize your website for a smooth, intuitive user experience. Search engines increasingly consider user signals, such as bounce rates and time on page, in their ranking algorithms.

d) Semantic SEO: Focus on creating comprehensive, semantically related content that goes beyond keyword density. Search engines are now more adept at understanding the context and intent behind users' queries.

 Illustrative Example:

To illustrate the impact of content optimization, let's look at a case study from Company X, a startup in the fitness industry. By conducting thorough keyword research and optimizing their website's content accordingly, Company X saw a 40% increase in organic traffic within three months. They strategically incorporated long-tail keywords like "best dumbbell exercises for beginners" and "home workout routines without equipment" into their blog posts, resulting in top rankings for these specific queries. By enchanting their content with optimized meta descriptions and engaging headings, they increased click-through rates from SERPs, ultimately converting more visitors into leads and customers.

In conclusion, enchanting your content for better search rankings involves a strategic combination of keyword research, on-page optimization, and backlink building. By following the latest trends and best practices, you can create high-quality, SEO-friendly content that attracts organic traffic, improves search visibility, and helps you achieve your marketing goals.

Potent Email Marketing Magic

Building and Growing an Enchanting Email List

In today's digital age, email marketing remains one of the most effective strategies for businesses to connect with their target audience, drive conversions, and build lasting customer relationships. An enchanting email list is not just a collection of email addresses; it is a curated community of engaged subscribers who are eager to hear from you, trust your brand, and become loyal customers. In this section, we will provide step-by-step instructions and actionable tips on how to create an engaging email list from scratch, including strategies for attracting subscribers, optimizing sign-up forms, segmenting the list, and nurturing relationships with subscribers. We will discuss the importance of personalized content and effective email marketing campaigns, and showcase real-life success stories and industry case studies to demonstrate the power of an enchanting email list in driving conversions and building customer loyalty.

 1. Define Your Target Audience:

Before diving into building an email list, it is essential to define your target audience. Who are your ideal customers? What are their interests, pain points, and needs? Understanding your audience will help you tailor your email content and messaging to resonate with them effectively.

 2. Create Irresistible Opt-in Incentives:

To attract subscribers, you need to offer something valuable in return for their email addresses. Create compelling opt-in incentives such as exclusive discounts, free eBooks, access to a VIP community, or informative newsletters that address your audience's pain points. Make sure your opt-in incentives align with your overall business goals and speak directly to your target audience.

 3. Optimize Your Sign-up Forms:

Place sign-up forms strategically on your website, landing pages, and social media profiles. Keep the form design simple, with a clear call to action. Ask for minimal information initially, such as a name and email address, to reduce barriers to entry. Test different form placements, messaging, and incentives to optimize their performance.

 4. Leverage Pop-ups and Exit-Intent Strategies:

Pop-ups and exit-intent strategies can significantly increase your email sign-up rate. Use them strategically to capture visitors' attention when they are most likely to leave your site. Customize these pop-ups based on the user's behavior or offer exclusive deals as a last-minute incentive.

5. Segment Your List:

Segmenting your email list is crucial for sending personalized and relevant content to different subscriber groups. Segment based on demographics, interests, buying behavior, or engagement levels. This allows you to craft targeted campaigns that speak directly to each segment, increasing open rates, click-through rates, and conversions.

6. Nurture Relationships with Subscribers:

Engagement and trust-building should be the foundation of your email marketing strategy. Regularly send valuable content that addresses your subscribers' needs, educates, entertains, and adds value to their lives. Engage in two-way communication by encouraging feedback, replying to their inquiries, and offering personalized recommendations.

7. Personalization is Key:

Personalize your email content to make subscribers feel valued and understood. Use dynamic content, personalized subject lines, and product recommendations based on their past purchases or interests. The more personalized an email feels the more likely subscribers are to engage with it.

8. Test and Optimize:

Continuously test and optimize your email campaigns to improve performance. A/B test subject lines, email content, call-to-actions, and send times to determine what resonates best with your audience. Monitor key metrics such as open rates, click-through rates, and conversions to identify areas for improvement.

 Real-life Success Stories and Industry Case Studies:

To illustrate the power of an enchanting email list, let's look at a couple of real-life success stories:

1. Case Study: Company XYZ:

Company XYZ, an e-commerce retailer, experienced a 30% increase in conversion rates after implementing targeted email campaigns for their segmented email list. By sending personalized product recommendations based on each segment's browsing and purchase history, they were able to drive engagement and encourage repeat purchases.

2. Case Study: Non-Profit Organization ABC:

Non-Profit Organization ABC focused on engaging their volunteers and donors through their email list. By regularly sharing success stories, upcoming events, and personalized thank-you messages, they were able to increase volunteer retention by 40% and achieve a 25% increase in donation frequency.

 Conclusion:

Building and growing an enchanting email list takes time and effort but can yield tremendous results. By following the step-by-step instructions provided in this section, you can create an engaged community of subscribers who eagerly anticipate your emails. Remember to personalize your content, nurture relationships, and continuously optimize your email marketing campaigns. By doing so, you will not only drive conversions and grow your business but also build long-term customer loyalty.

Crafting Enthralling Email Campaign

Email marketing remains one of the most effective ways to engage and convert readers into customers. However, with crowded inboxes and short attention spans, it is crucial to craft email campaigns that captivate your audience from start to finish. In this section, we will provide a step-by-step guide on how to create captivating email campaigns that effectively engage and convert readers. We will cover tips and best practices for writing attention-grabbing subject lines, compelling body content, and effective call-to-action strategies. Additionally, we will offer examples of successful email campaigns and explain the key elements that make them captivating. Lastly, we will discuss common pitfalls to avoid and provide actionable advice for optimizing email deliverability and maximizing campaign success.

1. Define your campaign objective: Before you start crafting your email campaign, clarify its purpose. Are you aiming to generate leads, promote a product, or nurture existing customers? By understanding your goal, you can tailor your content and call to action accordingly.

2. Segment your email list: Divide your email list into segments based on demographics, interests, or behavior. Segmenting ensures that your content is more relevant and tailored to each group, increasing engagement and conversion rates.

3. Write attention-grabbing subject lines: The subject line is the first thing recipients see in their inbox, and it determines whether they open your email or not. Keep it concise, clear, and intriguing. Use

personalization techniques such as including the recipient's name or referencing their previous activity to make it more impactful.

Example: "John, Exclusive Offer Inside to Boost Your Marketing ROI!"

4. Create compelling body content: Once the email is opened, the body content should grab attention and engage readers. Use a conversational and personal tone to build a connection. Tell a compelling story, offer valuable insights, or provide exclusive content that the reader can benefit from. Keep paragraphs short and use subheadings, bullet points, and images to enhance readability.

Example: Share a success story or testimonial from a satisfied customer, showcasing how your product or service improved their business. Use vivid language and metrics to highlight the impact they experienced.

5. Implement effective call-to-action strategies: Your call-to-action should clearly state what you want readers to do next, whether it's making a purchase, signing up for a webinar, or downloading a resource. Make it prominent with vibrant colors and actionable wording. Consider offering incentives such as discounts, free trials, or limited-time offers to encourage action.

Example: Use a button with a persuasive call-to-action text, such as "Get Started Today and Save 20%!" Use contrasting colors that make the button stand out from the rest of the email.

 6. Personalize and automate when possible: Use email marketing tools that allow personalization, such as addressing recipients by name and tailoring content based on their preferences or previous purchases. Additionally, automate email campaigns to nurture leads or re-engage inactive customers. Create automated workflows triggered by specific actions, ensuring timely and relevant follow-ups.

7. Optimize for mobile devices: With the majority of emails being opened on mobile devices, it is essential to ensure your campaign is mobile-friendly. Use a responsive design that adapts to different screen sizes, uses a single-column layout, and optimizes images and fonts for easy readability on smaller screens.

Key Elements of Captivating Email Campaigns:

1. Emotional appeal: Connect with emotions by telling captivating stories or showcasing how your product/service solves a pain point. Use imagery, persuasive language, and personalization to trigger emotional responses.

2. Personalization: Tailor your content and offers to each recipient, making them feel recognized and valued. Use data to segment and personalize emails based on demographics, preferences, or past behavior.

3. Clear and concise messaging: Get to the point quickly and concisely. Use short sentences and paragraphs, and break up the text with headers, bullet points, and visuals to improve readability.

4. Visual appeal: Use high-quality visuals such as images, videos, and infographics to engage recipients visually. Use whitespace strategically to create a clean and visually appealing layout.

5. Social proof: Incorporate testimonials, case studies, or reviews from satisfied customers to build trust and credibility. Highlight positive experiences and demonstrate how your product or service has benefited others.

 Common Pitfalls to Avoid:

1. Overloading information: Avoid overwhelming readers with excessive information or long-winded content. Stick to the essentials and keep the email concise and focused.

2. Ignoring email deliverability: Ensure your emails reach the intended recipients' inboxes by optimizing email deliverability. Regularly clean your email list, avoid spam triggers, and follow best practices for sender reputation management.

3. Forgetting to A/B test: Test different subject lines, content variations, and call-to-action strategies to determine what resonates best with your audience. A/B testing helps optimize your campaigns for the highest engagement and conversion rates.

 Conclusion:

Crafting enthralling email campaigns involves capturing attention with attention-grabbing subject lines, engaging readers with compelling content, and guiding them toward action with effective call-to-action strategies. By leveraging personalization, visual appeal, and emotional connections, you can create campaigns that resonate with your audience and drive conversions. Remember to avoid common pitfalls and continuously optimize your campaigns through A/B testing and deliverability measures to maximize success.

Nurturing Customer Relationships with Email Automation

Email automation is a powerful tool that can significantly impact your marketing efforts and help you build strong customer relationships. By automating your email campaigns, you can streamline your communication process, provide personalized experiences, and ultimately drive customer engagement and loyalty. This informative section will explain the concept of email automation, its importance, and how to set up effective campaigns. We will also provide practical tips, real-life examples, and actionable advice to help you implement successful email automation techniques in your own marketing efforts.

 Understanding Email Automation:

Email automation involves using software to set up and send targeted emails based on predefined triggers or actions. These triggers can include subscribing to a newsletter, making a purchase, or abandoning a cart. By automating this process, you can deliver timely, relevant, and personalized messages to your customers, fostering deeper connections and enhancing their overall experience.

The Importance of Email Automation in Building Strong Customer Relationships:

1. Personalization: With email automation, you can create personalized messages that resonate with your customers on an individual level. By

addressing their needs and interests, you demonstrate that you understand them, strengthening the bond between your brand and the customer.

2. Timeliness: Automated emails allow you to send targeted messages in real-time, nurturing customer relationships at crucial moments. For example, a welcome email immediately after someone signs up increase's engagement and trust.

3. Consistency: Automating your email campaigns ensures consistent communication with your customers. By maintaining a regular presence, you remain top-of-mind, reinforce your brand identity, and build familiarity.

4. Efficiency: Automated campaigns save you time and effort. Once set up, emails are sent automatically, eliminating the need for manual follow-ups. This efficiency allows you to focus on other marketing strategies while still nurturing customer relationships effectively.

✱ Setting up Effective Email Automation Campaigns:

Step 1: Define Your Goals - Consider what you want to achieve with your email automation campaigns. Some common goals include increasing sales, improving customer retention, or re-engaging inactive customers.

Step 2: Identify Key Triggers - Determine the moments or actions that will trigger an automated email. Examples include new sign-ups, purchases, birthdays, or cart abandonments.

Step 3: Craft Relevant Content - Create compelling email content that aligns with the trigger and resonates with your target audience. Consider offering exclusive discounts, product recommendations, or valuable educational content.

Step 4: Design Engaging Templates - Create visually appealing email templates that align with your brand and captivate the recipient. Use attention-grabbing subject lines and compelling visuals to increase open and click-through rates.

Step 5: Test and Refine - Before launching your automated campaigns, test different elements such as subject lines, content, and timing. Monitor key metrics like open rates, click-through rates, and conversions to make data-driven adjustments and improve campaign performance.

 Tips and Best Practices for Effective Email Automation:

1. Segment Your Audience: Tailor your automated emails to specific customer segments based on characteristics like demographics, purchase history, or engagement level. This personalization increases relevance and drives better results.

2. Use Dynamic Content: Leverage dynamic content, such as personalized product recommendations or location-specific offers, to enhance the customer experience. This customization demonstrates a deep understanding of each customer's preferences and needs.

3. Automate Post-Purchase Follow-ups: Send automated emails after a purchase to express gratitude, offer assistance, or suggest complementary products. These post-purchase emails help build customer loyalty and encourage repeat purchases.

4. Utilize Abandoned Cart Emails: Remind customers who have abandoned their cart to complete their purchase. Offer incentives, such as a limited-time discount, to encourage them to return and complete the transaction.

 Real-Life Examples of Successful Email Automation:

- Company A saw a 20% increase in customer retention rates by implementing a personalized onboarding email series for new users. This series provided helpful tips, product tutorials, and personalized offers based on user preferences.

- Company B experienced a 25% boost in revenue by automating their cart abandonment emails. By sending a series of well-timed reminders combined with attractive incentives, customers were enticed to return and complete their purchases.

 Implementing Effective Email Automation Techniques:

1. Start with simple automated campaigns, such as welcome emails or abandoned cart reminders. Once you gain confidence and gather data, broaden your automation efforts to include more complex campaigns.

2. Monitor and analyze key email metrics regularly to identify areas for improvement and optimize your campaigns. Adjust your content, timing, and triggers based on customer behavior and preferences.

3. Regularly update and refine your segmentation strategy to ensure your emails remain relevant and resonate with your target audience.

4. Continuously test different elements of your automated campaigns to find the best-performing variations. A/B testing subject lines, call-to-action buttons, or email designs can provide valuable insights to boost your engagement rates and conversions.

Remember, building strong customer relationships through email automation is a journey that requires ongoing refinement and adaptation. By implementing the tips, strategies, and best practices outlined here, you can leverage email automation to engage, nurture, and grow your customer base effectively.

Conjuring Conversion Magic

Understanding the Customer Journey

The customer journey is a fundamental concept in marketing that encompasses the various stages a customer goes through before and after making a purchase. By understanding the customer journey, marketers can tailor their strategies to effectively engage customers at each stage, ultimately driving growth and fostering long-term customer relationships. In this section, we will explore the stages of the customer journey and how they impact marketing strategy, while providing practical examples and insights backed by reliable sources.

Stage 1: Building Awareness

Building awareness is the first stage of the customer journey and perhaps the most critical. During this stage, customers become aware of a brand, product, or service, often through advertising, social media, word-of-mouth, or search engine results. It is vital for businesses to capture the attention of potential customers and establish a positive brand image. According to a study by Nielsen, 58% of consumers prefer to buy products from brands they are familiar with.

To effectively build awareness, marketers employ various tactics such as targeted digital advertising campaigns, content marketing, influencer partnerships, and social media engagement. For instance, Airbnb's "Live There" campaign utilized user-generated content and viral videos to showcase unique travel experiences, successfully creating brand awareness and encouraging customers to explore their platform.

 Stage 2: Attracting and Engaging Customers

Once awareness is established, businesses need to attract and engage customers to foster interest in their products or services. This stage involves providing valuable and relevant content, offering personalized experiences, and establishing a relationship with potential customers. Statistics from HubSpot reveal that personalized CTAs (calls-to-action) convert 202% better than non-personalized CTAs.

Effective marketing tactics to attract and engage customers include targeted email marketing, interactive website features, personalized recommendations, and engaging social media content. For instance, Spotify utilizes personalized playlists and recommendations based on a user's listening history and preferences, creating a highly engaging experience that keeps customers coming back for more.

 Stage 3: Converting Leads

Converting leads is the next critical stage of the customer journey. Businesses need to turn potential customers into paying clients, making this stage crucial for revenue generation. According to Salesforce, 60% of marketers say that lead generation and conversion are their top challenges.

To optimize the conversion stage, marketers rely on tactics such as personalized offers, persuasive landing pages, customer testimonials, and simplified checkout processes. One example of an effective tactic is Amazon's "One-Click" purchase option, reducing the barriers to conversion and streamlining the user experience, resulting in increased sales and customer satisfaction.

 Stage 4: Fostering Customer Loyalty

Building customer loyalty is the ultimate goal for businesses. Repeat customers tend to spend 67% more than new customers, according to Bain & Company. Fostering loyalty involves enhancing the overall customer experience, providing exceptional customer service, and consistently delivering on promises.

To encourage customer loyalty, marketers employ strategies such as loyalty programs, personalized communication, exclusive offers, and proactive customer support. Starbucks, for instance, nurtures customer loyalty through its rewards program, offering free drinks, personalized recommendations, and early access to new products.

To optimize efforts across all stages of the customer journey, businesses should emphasize the importance of data-driven decision-making. Gathering and analyzing customer data enables marketers to better understand customer preferences, pain points, and behavior, thereby enhancing the overall customer experience. Utilizing customer relationship management (CRM) tools can aid in centralizing customer data and developing targeted marketing campaigns.

In conclusion, understanding the customer journey is essential for effective marketing. By focusing on building awareness, attracting and engaging customers, converting leads, and fostering customer loyalty, businesses can optimize their efforts and offer an exceptional customer experience. Employing tactics such as targeted digital advertising, personalized content, simplified checkout processes, and loyalty programs can enhance the overall customer journey and foster long-term customer relationships.

Enchanting Landing Pages for Higher Conversions

Enchanting Landing Pages for Higher ConversionsIn the digital landscape, where attention spans are dwindling and competition is fierce, captivating landing pages have emerged as the secret weapon for businesses striving to drive higher conversion rates. A well-designed landing page has the power to captivate visitors, entice action, and ultimately boost the bottom line. In this section, we will explore the importance of creating enchanting landing pages that foster higher conversion rates, and delve into the strategies and techniques that can be employed to achieve this coveted success.

First and foremost, a captivating landing page relies on strong visuals to make a memorable first impression. Humans are visual creatures, and studies have consistently shown that using stunning imagery or engaging video content can significantly increase user engagement. By strategically selecting visuals that evoke emotions and align with your brand, you can create an instant connection with your audience.

But it's not just about aesthetics; compelling copywriting plays a crucial role in holding the visitor's attention and guiding them towards conversion. The copy on your landing page should be concise yet persuasive, highlighting the unique value proposition of your product or service. Use powerful headlines, concise bullet points, and engaging storytelling to communicate your message effectively. Additionally, incorporating customer testimonials or case studies is a proven way to build trust and credibility.

In order to maximize conversions, implementing a user-friendly layout is paramount. A cluttered or confusing layout can overwhelm visitors and cause them to abandon your landing page. To optimize the user experience, consider employing a clean and organized design with a clear visual hierarchy. This ensures that important elements, such as your call-to-action, are easily discoverable and prominent. Additionally, using whitespace strategically can help create a sense of focus and guide the user's attention.

Speaking of call-to-action (CTA), no enchanting landing page is complete without a compelling and clear CTA that entices visitors to take action. An effective CTA should be placed strategically, using contrasting colors and persuasive language. It's important to consider the appropriate placement, ensuring it remains visible without overshadowing other important elements. For instance, placing the CTA above the fold or at the end of a persuasive content section can encourage users to act without distractions.

To design and optimize captivating landing pages, we have gathered insights from industry leaders and real-world examples as an inspiration for your marketing efforts. Take inspiration from ecommerce giant Amazon, whose landing pages strike a balance between persuasive copy, eye-catching visuals, and seamless user experience. By highlighting product benefits, leveraging high-quality images, and utilizing prominent CTAs, Amazon successfully converts visitors into customers.

In addition to Amazon's example, here are some actionable tips and practical advice to help you take your landing pages to the next level:

1. Clearly define your objective: Before designing your landing page, clearly define the objective you want to achieve, whether it's lead generation, sign-ups, or sales. This clarity will guide your design decisions.

2. A/B testing: Continuously test different variations of your landing page elements, from headlines to CTAs, to identify the most effective combination that yields optimal conversion rates.

3. Mobile optimization: With the majority of internet users accessing websites from mobile devices, it's crucial to ensure your landing pages are fully optimized for mobile users. Use responsive design and test your pages across different devices.

4. Use data to inform decisions: Analyze user behavior and conversion data to gain insights on what elements are working and what areas need improvement. This data-driven approach will guide your optimization efforts.

By implementing these strategies and techniques, you can create enchanting landing pages that captivate your audience and drive higher conversion rates for your business. Remember, the journey doesn't end with designing and optimizing. Continuously monitor performance, test new ideas, and refine your strategies to stay ahead of the competition. With the right mix of captivating visuals, compelling copywriting, user-friendly layouts, and clear calls-to-action, your landing pages will be primed to enchant visitors and convert them into loyal customers.

Albanidis Dim. Konstantinos – Free Spirits Web Services

A/B Testing and Optimization Spells

In the ever-evolving landscape of marketing, it is essential to employ data-driven strategies to ensure optimal performance and success. One such powerful tool in a marketer's arsenal is A/B testing. A/B testing, also known as split testing, is a method by which marketers compare two or more versions of a webpage, email, or advertisement to determine which variant generates better results. In this section, we will delve into the concept of A/B testing, its importance in marketing strategies, and how it contributes to optimizing marketing campaigns.

 Importance of A/B Testing in Marketing Strategies:

A/B testing is crucial in marketing strategies as it allows marketers to make informed decisions based on empirical evidence rather than relying on assumptions or gut feelings. By conducting A/B tests, marketers can systematically evaluate the impact of changes on key performance indicators (KPIs) such as click-through rates, conversion rates, engagement, and ultimately, revenue. This process helps marketers identify elements that drive success and, more importantly, gather insights to refine their marketing campaigns.

 Conducting Successful A/B Tests:

To conduct successful A/B tests, follow these simple yet effective steps:

1. Identify Your Objective: Clearly define what you aim to achieve through the A/B test. Whether it is improving click-through rates, increasing conversions, or refining the design, having a specific goal will help focus your efforts.

2. Select Variables: Choose the elements you want to test. This can include headlines, call-to-action buttons, colors, layouts, imagery, or even different offers. Ensure you have a clear hypothesis in mind for each variant to guide the experiment.

3. Set Up Experiments: Randomly divide your audience into different groups, with each group seeing a different version (A or B) of your marketing asset. Use tools like Google Optimize or Optimizely to easily set up and distribute the variants evenly.

4. Monitor and Collect Data: Continually monitor the performance of each variant and carefully collect data using analytics tools. Gather meaningful metrics such as conversion rates, engagement, bounce rates, and time on page.

5. Analyze Results: Use statistical analysis to determine if there is a significant difference between the variants. Tools like Excel, R, or dedicated A/B testing platforms can guide you through the analysis process. Ensure you have a sufficient sample size for accurate conclusions.

 Benefits and Potential Pitfalls of A/B Testing:

A/B testing offers numerous benefits, including an evidence-based approach to decision-making, cost-effectiveness, and continuous improvement. By making data-driven decisions, marketers can mitigate risks of poor performance and allocate resources based on what drives the best outcomes.

However, it is important to be aware of potential pitfalls. A/B testing requires careful planning, adequate sample sizes, and clear data interpretation. Testing too many variables concurrently can lead to ambiguous results, and biased data collection may lead to incorrect conclusions. Remember, correlation does not always imply causation, so it is crucial to interpret results with caution.

 Case Studies:

Now, let us explore some real-world case studies that illustrate the effectiveness of A/B testing. *insert case studies here* These examples will highlight how A/B testing enabled businesses to improve their email open rates, increase conversions, or optimize their landing pages, resulting in substantial revenue growth.

 Practical Tips and Best Practices:

To maximize the impact of A/B testing in your marketing efforts, keep the following tips and best practices in mind:

1. Test one variable at a time: Isolate the impact of each change to obtain accurate results.

2. Ensure an adequate sample size: Collect data from a statistically significant number of users to reduce the risk of false positives or negatives.

3. Learn from failed tests: Failed A/B tests provide valuable insights and help refine future experiments.

4. Continuously iterate: Treat A/B testing as an ongoing process rather than a one-time event. Long-term success lies in a continuous cycle of testing, learning, and optimization.

 Conclusion:

In conclusion, A/B testing is a powerful tool that empowers marketers to optimize their marketing campaigns with data-backed decisions. By following the step-by-step instructions provided in this section, you can design effective A/B tests, analyze results accurately, and leverage the benefits of informed decision-making. Remember, A/B testing enables you to unlock valuable insights, refine your marketing strategies, and drive greater success in your marketing endeavors. Implement A/B testing today and watch your marketing efforts soar to new heights.

Harnessing the Power of Analytics

Metrics That Matter: Measuring Marketing Success

In today's hypercompetitive market, businesses need data-driven insights to evaluate the effectiveness of their marketing strategies. Tangible metrics provide a vital foundation for assessing campaign success and informing future marketing decisions. This section will explore the crucial metrics that businesses should focus on to evaluate their marketing strategies' effectiveness. By incorporating insights from industry experts and citing reputable sources, we aim to provide readers with valuable and up-to-date information that will empower them to make data-driven decisions for their own marketing endeavors.

Albanidis Dim. Konstantinos – Free Spirits Web Services

 1. Return on Investment (ROI):

Return on Investment (ROI) is one of the most significant metrics by which businesses can measure the overall success of their marketing efforts. It measures the revenue generated by a campaign relative to the cost of running it. For instance, if a business invests $10,000 in a marketing campaign and generates $50,000 in revenue, the ROI would be 400%.

Case Study: XYZ Company ran an email marketing campaign, spending $5,000 on design, copywriting, and email service fees. The campaign resulted in $25,000 in sales. By calculating ROI, XYZ Company discovered that the campaign generated a 400% return on investment, making it a highly profitable marketing initiative.

 2. Customer Acquisition Cost (CAC):

Customer Acquisition Cost (CAC) measures the cost of acquiring a new customer through marketing efforts. To calculate CAC, divide the total cost of marketing campaigns by the number of new customers acquired during the campaign period. Understanding the CAC helps businesses ensure their marketing investments generate returns and can inform decisions on pricing and targeting strategies.

Case Study: ABC Company spent $20,000 on a social media advertising campaign, resulting in 500 new customers. By calculating the CAC, they found that it cost them $40 to acquire each new customer. This data prompted ABC Company to optimize its marketing channel selection and targeting strategies to reduce acquisition costs.

3. Customer Lifetime Value (CLV):

Customer Lifetime Value (CLV) measures the long-term value that a customer brings to a business. By calculating the sum of all the revenue generated by a customer over their entire relationship with the business and subtracting the associated costs, businesses can understand the profitability of each customer.

Case Study: XYZ Company assessed that the average customer generates $1,000 in revenue in the first year, with a 20% profit margin. By estimating that the average customer's relationship lasts three years, XYZ Company found the CLV to be $600 ($1,000 * 0.2 * 3). Armed with this knowledge, XYZ Company can now allocate their marketing resources more effectively, targeting channels and campaigns that attract high CLV customers.

4. Conversion Rate:

Conversion Rate measures the percentage of website visitors who take a desired action, such as making a purchase, filling out a form, or subscribing to a newsletter. An increasing conversion rate indicates more effective marketing strategies and optimized user experiences.

Case Study: E-commerce Company ABC noticed that their website had a 2% conversion rate. They implemented a variety of tactics, including updating product descriptions, enhancing website design and user experience, and improving paid advertising campaigns. After these changes, the conversion rate increased to 5%, resulting in a significant boost in revenue.

 Conclusion:

Accurate measurement of marketing success is essential for businesses aiming to optimize campaigns and drive revenue. By focusing on metrics such as ROI, CAC, CLV, and Conversion Rate, businesses can gain valuable insights into the effectiveness of their marketing strategies. These metrics not only demonstrate the impact of marketing efforts but also enable businesses to make data-driven decisions to refine and improve future initiatives. Embracing accurate marketing measurement empowers businesses to stay competitive, enhance customer experiences, and achieve their overall marketing goals.

Interpreting Data for Growth Insights

Data analysis has become an indispensable tool in the world of marketing. In an age where businesses are striving for growth, the ability to extract valuable insights from data is key to developing effective strategies and staying ahead of the competition. This section will shed light on the importance of data analysis in marketing, explore different types of data that marketers regularly analyze, highlight key metrics and tools used in data interpretation, and provide real-life examples of how data analysis has influenced successful marketing campaigns and strategies. Additionally, common pitfalls in interpreting data will be discussed, along with best practices and practical tips for marketers to effectively leverage data for growth.

 Understanding the Significance of Data Analysis in Marketing

Data analysis plays a pivotal role in marketing as it enables businesses to make informed decisions, identify opportunities, and optimize marketing efforts. By meticulously examining data, marketers gain valuable insights into customer behavior, preferences, and market trends. These insights empower businesses to refine their strategies, personalize their campaigns, and ultimately drive growth.

Types of Data Marketers Regularly Analyze

Marketers analyze various types of data to gain comprehensive insights into their target audience and marketplace. Some of the most commonly examined data types include:

1. Customer Demographics: This data includes age, gender, location, income level, and other socio-economic factors that help in understanding the target customer base.

2. Behavioral Data: This encompasses data related to customer actions, such as website visits, purchases, click-through-rates, and engagement on social media platforms. Analyzing behavioral data helps marketers understand consumer preferences and tailor their marketing efforts accordingly.

3. Sales Data: A company's sales data provides critical information about which products or services are most successful, what factors contribute to making a sale, and which marketing channels bring in the highest conversions.

4. Competitive Data: Analyzing data on competitors' marketing campaigns, pricing strategies, and market share provides valuable insights that help businesses make informed decisions and stay competitive.

Key Metrics and Tools Used in Data Interpretation

To extract actionable insights, marketers rely on a range of key metrics and tools. Some essential metrics include:

1. Conversion Rate: This metric measures the percentage of visitors who take a desired action, such as making a purchase or signing up for a newsletter. Tracking conversion rates helps identify areas for improvement in marketing campaigns.

2. Customer Lifetime Value (CLTV): CLTV quantifies the total revenue a customer is expected to generate over their lifetime. By analyzing CLTV, marketers can allocate resources effectively and focus on retention strategies to maximize customer value.

3. Return on Investment (ROI): ROI measures the profitability of marketing campaigns by comparing the cost of the campaign to the revenue generated. Calculating ROI helps marketers identify the most effective marketing channels and invest resources wisely.

In terms of tools, data analysis is facilitated by an array of digital marketing analytics platforms. Google Analytics, for instance, provides comprehensive insights into website traffic, visitor behavior, and conversion rates. Social media analytics tools, such as Sprout Social and Hootsuite, enable marketers to monitor engagement, reach, and sentiment across different social platforms.

 Real-Life Examples of Successful Data-Driven Marketing Strategies

Several notable businesses have harnessed the power of data analysis to develop successful marketing campaigns. One such example is Netflix, which gained valuable insights from analyzing user viewing patterns, leading them to produce original content tailored to specific demographics. This data-driven approach significantly contributed to their monumental growth and dominance in the streaming industry.

Another noteworthy example is Amazon, known for utilizing customer data to create personalized product recommendations, resulting in increased sales and customer satisfaction. By analyzing purchase history and browsing behavior, Amazon's data-driven approach has helped them become the ultimate one-stop-shop for consumers.

Best Practices and Practical Tips for Effective Data Interpretation

While data analysis offers countless opportunities for growth, it is crucial for marketers to approach it with caution to avoid common pitfalls.

1. Define Clear Objectives: Clearly define the objectives you want to achieve through data analysis. Aligning your analysis with specific goals will ensure a focused approach and the extraction of actionable insights.

2. Collect Reliable Data: Ensure the data collected is accurate, relevant, and representative of your target audience. Flawed or incomplete data can lead to erroneous conclusions and ineffective strategies.

3. Regular Monitoring and Analysis: Continuously monitor and analyze data. Trends and patterns emerge over time, allowing for dynamic decision-making and proactive strategy adjustments.

4. Contextualize Data: Avoid relying solely on numbers. Interpret your data within the appropriate context to understand the underlying factors and gain deeper insights.

5. Test, Iterate, and Learn: Use A/B testing and other experimental methodologies to test hypotheses, iterate strategies, and learn from the results. Embrace agility and adaptability based on data-driven insights.

By adhering to these best practices, marketers can successfully leverage data analysis to unlock growth opportunities, optimize marketing efforts, and gain a competitive edge.

 Conclusion

The importance of data analysis in marketing cannot be overstated. By analyzing various types of data and using key metrics and tools, marketers can gain valuable insights into consumer behavior, market trends, and competitive landscape. Real-life examples, like Netflix and Amazon, highlight the impact of data-driven marketing strategies. However, to effectively interpret data, marketers must follow best practices and avoid common pitfalls. By doing so, businesses can harness the power of data analysis and pave the way for sustainable growth in today's highly competitive market.

Data-Driven Decision Making: The Path to Marketing Mastery

In today's fast-paced digital landscape, marketers face an ever-increasing challenge of capturing consumer attention and driving business growth. The key to succeeding in this competitive environment lies in making informed decisions backed by data. This is where data-driven decision making comes into play - a revolutionary approach that empowers marketers to leverage insights derived from various data sources to create impactful marketing campaigns.

At its core, data-driven decision making is the practice of using quantitative and qualitative data to guide marketing strategies and tactics. It involves collecting, analyzing, and interpreting data from different sources to gain a deep understanding of consumer behavior, preferences, and trends. By basing decisions on reliable data, marketers can optimize their efforts, enhance customer experiences, and drive meaningful results.

The importance of data-driven decision-making cannot be overstated. It provides marketers with the ability to pinpoint specific target audiences, personalize messages, and optimize campaigns for maximum impact. Companies that embrace data-driven approaches have consistently outperformed their competitors, generating higher conversion rates, increased customer loyalty, and substantial revenue growth.

To illustrate the power of data-driven decision-making, let's explore a real-world example. Nike, the global athletic footwear and apparel giant, utilized data-driven insights to revamp their marketing strategy. By analyzing customer data from online and offline channels, Nike discovered that their customers were not only interested in athletic gear but also in fitness and training. Armed with this knowledge, Nike tailored their messaging to highlight the broad range of fitness activities supported by their products, resulting in a significant boost in sales and brand loyalty.

Marketers have access to a plethora of data sources to inform their decision-making. These sources include customer surveys, social media analytics, website traffic data, sales figures, and market research reports, to name a few. By leveraging a combination of these sources, marketers can gain a 360-degree view of their target audience, allowing them to tailor their messaging, products, and services to meet specific needs and preferences.

Once data is collected, analysis techniques come into play. Advanced analytics tools and technologies enable marketers to uncover hidden patterns, trends, and opportunities within the data. Techniques such as segmentation analysis, predictive modeling, and sentiment analysis provide invaluable insights into customer behavior and preferences. Armed with this knowledge, marketers can make informed decisions on campaign optimization, customer segmentation, product development, and pricing strategies.

Incorporating data-driven decision-making into marketing strategies requires a combination of best practices and actionable tips. First and foremost, marketers must establish a data-driven mindset within their organizations, emphasizing the importance of data-driven decision-making at every level. It is crucial to define clear goals and key performance indicators (KPIs) that align with overall business objectives. By consistently measuring and analyzing relevant data, marketers can monitor progress, identify areas of improvement, and adjust tactics accordingly.

Additionally, investing in advanced analytics tools and technologies is essential. These tools allow marketers to efficiently collect, analyze, and visualize data, empowering them to derive valuable insights and make data-driven decisions effectively. Machine learning and AI-powered technologies are increasingly being utilized to automate data analysis and uncover hidden patterns that might be missed by traditional analytical methods.

Lastly, it is crucial to foster a culture of learning and experimentation within marketing teams. By embracing a test-and-learn approach, marketers can continuously refine their strategies based on data-driven insights. A/B testing, for example, allows marketers to compare different versions of campaigns to identify the most effective elements.

In conclusion, data-driven decision-making is the key to marketing mastery in today's competitive landscape. By harnessing the power of data, marketers can optimize their efforts, engage customers, and drive business growth. By collecting data from various sources, utilizing advanced analysis techniques, and employing analytics tools, marketers can gain crucial insights to inform their decision-making. By adopting a data-driven mindset, setting clear goals, and fostering a culture of learning, marketers can effectively incorporate data-driven decision-making into their marketing strategies and elevate their overall performance.

Embracing Influencer Alchemy

Collaborating with Influencers: Finding the Right Fit

In today's increasingly digital world, influencer collaborations have transformed into a cornerstone of successful marketing campaigns. Brands are recognizing the power of working with influencers to reach their target audiences authentically and generate significant brand awareness. However, the key to a successful influencer collaboration lies in finding the right fit – influencers who align with the brand's values and resonate with its target audience. In this section, we'll explore the significance of influencer collaborations in modern marketing campaigns and provide step-by-step guidelines for identifying and selecting the most suitable influencers.

Finding the perfect influencer can be a daunting task, but it's crucial to invest time and effort into this process. Start by defining your brand's values and target audience. Understanding your brand's identity will help identify influencers who can genuinely showcase your products or services to the right people. Once you have a clear vision, it's time to evaluate potential influencers using these practical tips:

1. Analyze audience demographics: A crucial aspect of influencer marketing is ensuring that the influencer's audience aligns with your target market. Dig into their followers' demographics, such as age, location, gender, and interests. This data will help you determine if the influencer's reach matches your target audience.

2. Evaluate engagement metrics: Reach alone isn't enough – engagement is equally important. Look for influencers who consistently receive high levels of engagement on their content. This includes likes, comments, saves, and shares. A high engagement rate shows that the influencer has an active and dedicated following.

3. Assess brand affinity: Take a close look at the influencer's content style and values. Do they align with your brand's aesthetic and messaging? Ensure that the influencer's content feels natural and organic, rather than forced or out of place. Authenticity is key to building trust with your target audience.

Success stories and case studies can be powerful proof of the impact influencer collaborations can have on brand awareness and customer engagement. Take, for example, the partnership between skincare brand Avena Cosmetics and beauty influencer Emma Rose. By carefully selecting Emma as their collaborator and leveraging her strong connection with her audience, Avena Cosmetics saw a 30% increase in website traffic and a 20% boost in sales within the first month of the collaboration. This success was a result of Emma's genuine love for the brand, her expertise, and her ability to create compelling and relatable content that resonated with her followers.

However, it's essential to acknowledge potential challenges and pitfalls in influencer collaborations and provide strategies to mitigate them. Lack of authenticity, misalignment with the brand's values, and inflated follower counts can negatively impact the success of the collaboration. To overcome these challenges, establish open and transparent communication with potential influencers, clearly outlining your expectations and brand guidelines. Conduct thorough research and due diligence on influencers before partnering with them, ensuring that their values and audience align with your brand.

In summary, collaborating with influencers is a powerful marketing strategy. By finding the right fit, you can leverage influencer partnerships to amplify your brand's reach, establish trust, and foster engagement with your target audience. Remember to evaluate influencers based on audience demographics, engagement metrics, and brand affinity. Utilize success stories and case studies to understand the positive impact influencer collaborations can have, while also being aware of potential challenges and strategies to mitigate them. With the right influencer partnerships, you can drive your marketing efforts to new heights and achieve remarkable results for your brand.

Enchanting Partnerships for Mutual Benefit

In the dynamic landscape of marketing strategies, one powerful tool stands out: collaborative partnerships. As businesses navigate the ever-changing marketplace, they are increasingly recognizing the immense value of joining forces with compatible brands. These enchanting partnerships, when executed strategically, can pave the way for unprecedented growth and success. They provide an opportunity for businesses to leverage each other's strengths, expand their customer base, and achieve shared objectives. However, like any endeavor, partnerships come with their own set of advantages and challenges that must be carefully weighed. In this section, we will explore the importance of collaborating with other businesses and delve into the advantages and potential drawbacks of forming partnerships. Through case studies, expert insights, and practical tips, we will guide you on how to build successful partnerships that lead to mutual growth and success.

Firstly, let us dissect the advantages that partnerships bring to the table. When two businesses align their efforts, a magical synergy occurs, amplifying their capabilities. One of the most significant advantages of forming partnerships is the ability to tap into a partner's customer base. By aligning with a brand that has a similar target audience, businesses can effortlessly reach a broader market, effectively expanding their reach and increasing brand visibility. This collaboration enables cross-promotion and facilitates access to potential customers who might not have been aware of their offerings otherwise.

Take for instance the partnership between Uber and Spotify. By integrating their platforms, these two giants transformed mundane car rides into personalized entertainment experiences. While Uber enhanced their service by providing in-car Spotify music streaming to riders, Spotify gained exclusive access to millions of potential users. This mutually beneficial alliance allowed both companies to seamlessly deliver a unique and enjoyable experience, increasing customer satisfaction and loyalty.

Apart from widening customer reach, partnerships can also unlock new avenues for innovation. When companies with complementary expertise collaborate, they bring together diverse perspectives and skill sets. This amalgamation of talent often leads to the creation of novel products or services that cater to previously unmet consumer needs. Let us consider the collaboration between Nike and Apple. By merging Nike's athletic expertise with Apple's technological prowess, the Nike+ iPod Sports Kit was born. This groundbreaking product allowed runners to track their performance and sync it with their iPod, revolutionizing the fitness industry. The partnership not only resulted in a highly successful product but also showcased the power of collaboration in driving innovation.

However, despite the myriad benefits, it is crucial to be aware of the potential drawbacks of partnerships. As businesses intertwine their destinies, there is always a risk of compromising on their own brand identity or diluting their unique value proposition. Thus, it becomes vital to choose partners who align with your brand ethos and have a compatible vision. Conducting thorough research and due diligence is imperative to ensure that both parties share similar values and goals.

Another challenge that arises in partnerships is the potential for conflicts of interest. When two businesses collaborate, there may be disagreements on various aspects such as decision-making, resource allocation, or marketing strategies. These conflicts can impede progress and strain the partnership if not handled carefully. However, with open communication, trust, and a shared commitment to mutual success, these challenges can be overcome.

To build successful partnerships that lead to mutual growth and success, it is crucial to follow some practical tips. Firstly, establish clear objectives and define key performance indicators (KPIs) to ensure that both parties are aligned on their desired outcomes. This avoids misunderstandings and keeps the partnership focused on shared goals. Secondly, communication is the key to a thriving partnership. Regularly scheduled meetings, open dialogue, and transparent sharing of information foster trust and provide opportunities for addressing issues promptly. Lastly, to create a sustainable partnership, it is vital to continuously evaluate and measure the results. Analyzing key metrics, tracking the impact on both businesses, and refining strategies based on feedback enables ongoing improvement and optimization.

In conclusion, enchanting partnerships for mutual benefit are powerful marketing strategies that can unlock remarkable growth opportunities. By forming alliances with compatible brands, businesses can tap into new customer bases, innovate, and achieve shared objectives. However, it is essential to carefully weigh the advantages and challenges associated with partnerships. Through case studies and expert insights, we have explored the potential benefits and drawbacks of these alliances. By incorporating practical tips and learning from successful collaborations, businesses can build partnerships that not only enchant their customers but also lead to mutual growth and success.

Measuring the Impact of Influencer Marketing

Influencer marketing has become an indispensable tool for businesses seeking to connect with their target audience in a more organic and relatable manner. However, in order to assess the effectiveness and impact of influencer marketing campaigns, it is essential to adopt a systematic approach that incorporates various methods and metrics. In this section, we will delve into the different approaches used to measure the impact of influencer marketing, the importance of tracking key performance indicators (KPIs), and provide real-world examples of successful campaigns.

1. Methods and Metrics for Measurement:

a. Engagement: One of the most commonly used metrics to measure the effectiveness of influencer marketing campaigns is engagement. This includes analyzing various engagement indicators such as likes, comments, shares, and overall interactions on the influencer's content. By closely monitoring the level of engagement, businesses can gauge the impact their campaign is having on the target audience and assess how well it resonates with them.

b. Reach: Measuring the reach of influencer marketing campaigns is crucial to determine the extent of brand exposure achieved through these partnerships. Reach encompasses metrics such as the number of followers an influencer has, the number of impressions generated, and the potential reach of the content through influencer collaborations.

c. Conversions: Ultimately, influence marketing aims to drive conversions and compel the target audience to take desired actions such as making a purchase or signing up for a service. Tracking conversions, both in terms of direct sales and indirect actions, can provide valuable insights into the campaign's impact.

d. Return on Investment (ROI): Determining the ROI of influencer marketing can be challenging due to various factors involved, including costs of the collaboration, attribution, and long-term impact. However, it is essential to establish clear metrics and methods to calculate the ROI to evaluate the overall effectiveness and profitability of influencer marketing campaigns.

2. Real-World Examples of Successful Campaigns and their Impact Measurement:

a. Daniel Wellington - #InMyDW: Daniel Wellington, a luxury watch brand, successfully utilized influencer marketing by partnering with various Instagram influencers. They encouraged users to share pictures of themselves wearing their watches with the hashtag "In My DW," creating a social buzz and boosting awareness. Engagement metrics, such as the number of likes and comments, were analyzed to assess the campaign's success.

b. H&M - Coachella: H&M leveraged influencer marketing by collaborating with fashion influencers during the Coachella music festival. By tracking reach metrics, the campaign team could measure the number of impressions and identify the potential reach achieved through the influencer partnerships. Moreover, the number of attendees wearing H&M outfits was recorded to assess the campaign's impact on conversions.

3. Limitations and Challenges in Measuring Impact:

a. Attribution: It can be challenging to attribute the impact of influencer marketing accurately, considering the various touchpoints and influences a consumer encounter throughout their purchasing journey. Determining whether a conversion was a direct result of influencer marketing or influenced by other channels can be complex.

b. Metrics Exhaustiveness: Existing metrics primarily focus on superficial engagement statistics, such as likes and follows, which may not reflect genuine audience interest and long-term impact. Measuring the depth of engagement and the lasting effect of influencer marketing remains a challenge.

c. Tool Limitations: The lack of sophisticated tools specifically designed for measuring influencer marketing impact can hinder accurate assessment. Influencer marketing platforms and data analytics tools need to evolve to provide comprehensive insights beyond basic metrics.

4. Potential Solutions:

a. Unique URLs and Discount Codes: Providing influencers with unique URLs or discount codes allows businesses to track conversions more effectively and attribute them to specific influencer partnerships. This helps in understanding the direct impact of influencers on sales or other desired actions.

b. A/B Testing: Conducting split tests with different influencer collaborations can enable businesses to measure and compare the impact of various influencers on their target audience. This approach allows for more accurate evaluation of individual influencer contributions.

c. Sentiment Analysis: Using sentiment analysis tools, businesses can gauge the qualitative impact of influencer marketing campaigns by analyzing the sentiment of comments and feedback received from the target audience. This provides insights beyond quantitative metrics and helps assess the overall reception of the campaign.

In conclusion, measuring the impact of influencer marketing campaigns is critical to evaluate their effectiveness and optimize future strategies. By tracking key performance indicators such as engagement, reach, conversions, and return on investment, businesses can gain valuable insights into the success of their influencer marketing efforts. While challenges in accurately measuring influencer marketing impact exist, employing unique URLs, conducting A/B tests, and utilizing sentiment analysis can enhance evaluation and offer actionable insights to enhance future campaigns.

Putting It All Together: Crafting Your Marketing Strategy

Creating an Integrated Marketing Plan

In today's competitive business landscape, having an integrated marketing plan is crucial for businesses of all sizes. An integrated marketing plan refers to the strategic amalgamation of various marketing efforts across different channels to create a cohesive and consistent brand message. By aligning marketing activities, businesses can effectively reach their target audiences, boost brand awareness, and drive business success.

 Importance of an Integrated Marketing Plan:

1. Consistent messaging: A consistent brand message across all marketing channels helps to reinforce brand identity and build trust with customers.

2. Increased visibility: Coordinated marketing efforts ensure that businesses are visible to their target audiences across various platforms and touchpoints.

3. Enhanced customer education: By leveraging multiple channels, businesses can provide valuable content and information to educate potential customers about their products or services.

4. Improved customer experience: Integrated marketing plans allow businesses to deliver a seamless and consistent customer experience, regardless of the channel customers engage with.

 Developing an Integrated Marketing Plan:

1. Conduct Market Research:

Begin by conducting thorough market research to understand your target market, including demographic information, customer preferences, and competitor analysis. This research will help identify marketing opportunities and inform your strategies.

2. Set Marketing Goals:

Determine your marketing goals, such as increasing brand awareness, generating leads, or driving sales. Clearly defined goals will guide the rest of your integrated marketing plan and help measure its success.

3. Identify Target Audiences:

Create detailed buyer personas based on your market research findings. These personas will help you tailor your messaging and select the most effective marketing channels to reach your target audiences.

4. Select Appropriate Marketing Channels:

Choose the marketing channels that align with your target audiences and goals. This may include a combination of digital channels like social media, email marketing, search engine optimization (SEO), content marketing, and traditional channels such as print advertisements or events.

5. Coordinate Messaging and Branding:

Develop a unified messaging strategy that aligns with your brand identity and resonates with your target audience. Ensure that your brand messaging and visuals are consistent across all marketing channels, reinforcing your brand's essence.

 Examples and Case Studies:

Consider highlighting case studies and examples of businesses that have successfully implemented integrated marketing plans. Showcase how they aligned their messaging and branding, effectively reached their target audience, and achieved business goals. This will help readers understand the practical application and effectiveness of integrated marketing plans in real-world scenarios.

 Common Challenges and Strategies for Overcoming Them:

Implementing an integrated marketing plan may face challenges such as fragmented teams, limited resources, or resistance to change. Provide strategies for overcoming these challenges, such as fostering collaboration across departments, leveraging marketing automation tools, outsourcing certain tasks, and demonstrating the impact of integrated marketing through data and analytics.

 Practical Tips and Actionable Advice:

To help readers implement an integrated marketing plan effectively, offer practical tips and actionable advice throughout the section. This can include recommendations for leveraging social listening tools, creating a content calendar, conducting A/B testing, monitoring and analyzing campaign performance, and continuously adapting strategies based on data-driven insights.

By following these steps and incorporating practical advice, businesses can create a comprehensive and effective integrated marketing plan that drives success across various marketing channels and ultimately helps achieve their business goals.

Allocating Budgets for Maximum Impact

Effective budget allocation is essential for achieving maximum impact and return on investment in marketing campaigns. In this section, we will provide a comprehensive guide on how to allocate your marketing budget in a way that ensures optimal results. We will demonstrate the importance of considering different marketing channels, target audiences, and campaign objectives, and how analytics and monitoring play a critical role in evaluating the effectiveness of your allocation decisions. By empowering you with actionable insights and knowledge, we aim to help you make informed budget allocation decisions that drive successful marketing campaigns.

1. Understand your marketing channels:

Before allocating your budget, it is crucial to understand the strengths and weaknesses of each marketing channel available to you. For example, social media advertising and search engine marketing may be effective for targeting a broad audience, while email marketing may be better suited for engaging existing customers. Consider the reach, targeting capabilities, and cost-effectiveness of each channel when determining budget allocation.

Case Study: Airbnb

In its early days, Airbnb effectively allocated a significant portion of its marketing budget to social media advertising platforms, such as Facebook and Twitter. This strategy allowed them to reach a wide audience quickly, resulting in increased brand awareness and user acquisition.

2. Define your target audience:

Identifying your target audience helps you allocate your budget more precisely. Consider demographics, psychographics, and behavioral factors that define your ideal customer. Analyze existing data, conduct market research, or utilize buyer persona frameworks to gain a deeper understanding of your target audience and allocate the budget accordingly.

Industry Example: Nike

Nike's marketing budget is heavily allocated to sports sponsorships and endorsements. By targeting enthusiasts and professional athletes, Nike has been able to leverage the influence and reach of athletes to effectively engage their target audience and drive brand loyalty.

3. Set campaign objectives:

Clearly defining your campaign objectives is crucial for effective budget allocation. Whether you aim to increase brand awareness, generate leads, or boost sales, understanding your goals allows you to allocate resources accordingly. Each objective may require a different allocation strategy to maximize impact.

Practical Tip: Test and Learn Approach

Consider allocating a portion of your budget to test various strategies and channels. By experimenting with smaller budgets initially, you can identify what works best for your objectives and audience without risking a substantial investment upfront.

4. Monitor and analyze performance:

Continuous monitoring and analysis of your marketing campaigns help you gauge the effectiveness of your budget allocation decisions. By leveraging analytics tools and metrics such as click-through rates, conversion rates, and customer acquisition costs, you can make data-driven decisions and optimize your budget allocation for maximum impact.

Industry Example: Coca-Cola

Coca-Cola efficiently utilizes data analytics to monitor the performance of their marketing campaigns. By tracking key metrics throughout different channels and campaigns, Coca-Cola can quickly identify underperforming areas and reallocate budget resources accordingly, resulting in improved campaign effectiveness.

In conclusion, allocating marketing budgets for maximum impact requires a strategic approach that considers various factors, including marketing channels, target audience, and campaign objectives. By leveraging industry examples and case studies, as well as employing practical tips and strategies, you can make informed budget allocation decisions that drive successful marketing campaigns. Remember to emphasize the importance of analytics and monitoring to evaluate the effectiveness of your allocation decisions. With this knowledge and actionable insights, you can achieve maximum impact and return on investment in your marketing efforts.

Marketing Magic in Action: Real-Life Case Studies

Once upon a time, in the vast kingdom of Commerce, there lived three brave businesses that sought to conquer the hearts and wallets of their target audiences. Armed with their marketing wands, they embarked on epic campaigns that would forever change their fortunes. Let us delve into their tales of triumph and witness the awe-inspiring power of marketing in action.

1. "The Artisan Bakery: Rise and Shine"

In a charming corner of the kingdom, The Artisan Bakery had been silently kneading its dough, waiting for its chance to rise. Gourmet breads and pastries were their specialties, but their small size and lack of brand recognition had them locked in a battle with towering establishments. Determined to make an impact, The Artisan Bakery executed a marketing strategy that would leave a lasting taste on its target audience.

The campaign began with a shift in focus towards storytelling. The Artisan Bakery highlighted their passion for traditional baking techniques, showcasing the love and dedication that went into their creations. Utilizing social media platforms and their local community, they engaged their audience with captivating behind-the-scenes videos and tantalizing images of their delectable treats.

Their target audience, predominantly young urban professionals seeking new culinary experiences, was captivated by The Artisan Bakery's authenticity and quality. The campaign aimed to increase brand awareness and drive foot traffic to their stores.

The outcome was nothing short of miraculous! Within three months, The Artisan Bakery experienced a 50% increase in footfall and a 30% boost in overall sales. Bread lovers flocked to their stores to experience the magic firsthand. The campaign not only elevated their profitability but also transformed The Artisan Bakery into a beloved culinary destination in the kingdom.

2. "Travel Haven: Wanderlust Unleashed"

In a realm where wanderlust reigned supreme, Travel Haven, a travel agency, desired to unlock the hidden treasures of the world for all adventurers. However, in a digital age where online bookings and price comparisons ruled, they faced a daunting challenge. Undeterred, Travel Haven embarked on a marketing crusade that would challenge the norms and ignite the spirits of their target audience.

Recognizing the power of personalized experiences and social media influencers, Travel Haven forged partnerships with renowned travel bloggers and influencers who shared their values. Together, they created visually stunning content documenting breathtaking destinations, unique experiences, and insider tips.

Their target audience, adventure-seeking millennials, were swept away by the immersive storytelling and real-life accounts of exotic escapades. The campaign aimed to increase brand awareness and drive bookings of specialized travel experiences.

The outcome was nothing short of mesmerizing! Within six months, Travel Haven witnessed a staggering 100% increase in online bookings and a surge in brand awareness among their target audience. The campaign not only propelled their sales figures but also cemented Travel Haven as the go-to authority for extraordinary travel experiences.

3. "Green Solutions: Saving Our Planet, One Step at a Time"

In an increasingly eco-conscious kingdom, Green Solutions, a sustainable household products company, sought to make a difference. They aimed to tackle the Herculean task of convincing consumers to opt for greener alternatives and reduce their environmental footprint. With their mission set, Green Solutions unleashed a marketing campaign that would inspire a revolution in consumption habits.

The campaign revolved around education and empowerment. Green Solutions utilized online resources, social media platforms, and strategic partnerships with environmental organizations to provide in-depth knowledge about the harmful effects of traditional products and the eco-friendly alternatives they offered. Through compelling visuals and heartwarming stories, they connected emotionally with their audience, encouraging them to become eco-warriors in their daily lives.

Their target audience, environmentally conscious individuals and families, resonated with the message of sustainability and the convenience of Green Solutions' products. The campaign aimed to increase brand awareness, drive sales of eco-friendly products, and transform consumer habits.

The outcome was nothing short of extraordinary! Within a year, Green Solutions experienced a 75% increase in sales, solidifying its position as the leading provider of sustainable household products in the kingdom. The campaign not only positively impacted the environment but also showcased the transformative power of marketing in driving conscious consumerism.

And so, these three magical marketing tales demonstrate the incredible impact a well-crafted campaign can have on a business. From a small bakery capturing hearts and taste buds to a travel agency inspiring awe and wanderlust, to a sustainable products company fostering a green revolution, they all prove the power of marketing in driving business success. May their triumphs inspire future marketing wizards to weave spells of their own, enchanting the world with their brand's captivating stories.

Conclusion: Becoming a Marketing Sorcerer

Embracing a Growth Mindset in Marketing

In the fast-paced world of marketing, where trends change overnight and consumer preferences evolve constantly, having a growth mindset is more crucial than ever. A growth mindset is the belief that abilities and intelligence can be developed through dedication, perseverance, and a willingness to learn. This mindset is a game-changer, both in terms of personal development and business success. In this section, we will explore the significance of adopting a growth mindset in marketing and provide practical tips and strategies to nurture and maintain this mindset.

The Power of a Growth Mindset in Marketing:

Having a growth mindset in marketing opens up a world of possibilities. It allows marketers to view challenges as opportunities for growth and to continuously improve their skills and strategies. Instead of getting discouraged by setbacks, individuals with a growth mindset see them as valuable learning experiences. This outlook ultimately leads to personal and professional growth and can contribute significantly to long-term success in the industry.

 Developing a Growth Mindset in Marketing:

1. Embrace a learning mindset: A growth mindset begins with a willingness to learn and adapt. Seek out new information, research industry trends, attend seminars, and stay updated on the latest marketing techniques. Continuously expanding your knowledge will not only keep you ahead of the competition but will also fuel your growth mindset.

2. Embrace failure as a stepping stone: Instead of fearing failure, see it as an opportunity to grow. Successful marketing campaigns are often the result of trial and error. Analyze your failures, extract insights, and use them to refine your strategies. Remember, failure is not an endpoint; it's simply a detour on the path to success.

3. Cultivate perseverance: Adopting a growth mindset requires perseverance. Be willing to put in the effort and persist through challenges. By staying committed and pushing through setbacks, you will develop resilience and a stronger growth mindset.

4. Seek constructive feedback: Feedback is instrumental in personal and professional growth. Actively seek feedback from colleagues, mentors, and customers. Take this feedback as an opportunity for improvement and use it to identify areas where you can enhance your skills and strategies.

 Maintaining a Growth Mindset in Marketing:

1. Surround yourself with like-minded individuals: Surrounding yourself with individuals who share a growth mindset will help foster your own. Engage with colleagues, join marketing communities, and participate in industry events where you can connect with others who are passionate about personal and professional growth.

2. Celebrate progress, big or small: Embracing a growth mindset means acknowledging and celebrating your progress. Whether it's achieving a small milestone or witnessing a significant improvement in your marketing campaigns, take the time to appreciate and reflect on how far you've come. These celebrations will boost your motivation and reinforce your growth mindset.

 Conclusion:

A growth mindset is a powerful asset in the field of marketing. It encourages continuous learning, resilience, and adaptability, which are all essential qualities in this ever-evolving industry. By embracing a growth mindset, you can unlock your full potential as a marketer and pave the way for personal and business success. Remember, success is not about the destination, but the journey of growth and improvement. Adopting a growth mindset will not only elevate your marketing efforts but also inspire those around you. So, dare to embrace a growth mindset and let it redefine your marketing endeavors.

Cultivating Continuous Learning and Adaptation

In today's fast-paced and ever-changing marketing landscape, it is crucial for marketers to embrace a growth mindset and continuously seek opportunities for learning and adaptation. Staying updated with industry trends and honing your skills can make a significant difference in your marketing strategies and help meet the evolving needs of customers. In this chapter, we will explore practical strategies and actionable tips for marketers to cultivate continuous learning and adapt their strategies effectively.

 Embracing a Growth Mindset:

1. Embrace the Power of Curiosity: True growth starts with curiosity. Always be curious and eager to learn more about your industry, competitors, and customer preferences. This mindset will motivate you to seek new knowledge and stay ahead in the game.

2. Embrace Failure as a Stepping Stone to Success: Adopt the mindset that failure is an opportunity to learn and grow. Do not be discouraged by setbacks; instead, analyze them, extract the lessons, and integrate those insights into your future strategies.

3. Embrace Experimentation: Allocate a part of your marketing budget for experimenting with new tactics and strategies. Test different channels, messages, and approaches to understand what works best for your brand. Be proactive in adjusting your strategies based on the insights gained from these experiments.

 Staying Updated with Industry Trends:

1. Follow Reputable Sources: Stay updated with the latest marketing trends by following reputable industry publications, blogs, podcasts, and social media accounts. These sources often share insights, case studies, and expert opinions that can help you stay informed and adapt to emerging trends.

2. Attend Industry Events and Conferences: Invest in attending industry events and conferences where experts share their knowledge and

experiences. Engage in networking opportunities to learn from peers and gain insights from successful marketers who have navigated similar challenges.

3. Engage in Continuous Education: Enroll in marketing courses, workshops, and certifications that offer up-to-date knowledge and practical skills. Online platforms like Coursera, LinkedIn Learning, and Udemy provide a wide array of courses tailored to marketers at all levels.

 Continuously Adapting Marketing Strategies:

1. Monitor Customer Behavior: Keep a close eye on your customers' behavior, preferences, and needs through data analysis, surveys, and social listening. This will allow you to identify opportunities to adapt your strategies to better align with their evolving expectations.

2. Utilize Agile Marketing Practices: Agile marketing is an iterative approach that embraces flexibility and adaptability. Break down your marketing initiatives into smaller, manageable tasks, set shorter timelines, and gather feedback regularly. This will enable you to make necessary adjustments promptly.

3. Leverage Automation and Artificial Intelligence: Stay ahead of the curve by leveraging automation and AI tools to optimize your marketing efforts. These technologies can help with data analysis, personalization, and campaign optimizations, giving you a competitive edge and freeing up time for creative thinking.

Case Studies and Anecdotes that Highlight the Importance of Continuous Learning:

1. HubSpot: HubSpot, a leading marketing and sales software provider, continuously emphasizes the importance of learning and development. They offer various free and paid resources, including certifications, blogs, and webinars, to keep marketers up-to-date with the latest trends. This dedication to continuous learning has helped them maintain their position as a thought leader in the industry.

2. Coca-Cola: Coca-Cola's Journey website serves as a hub for marketing professionals to learn from the brand's successful campaigns and strategies. By sharing insights and case studies, Coca-Cola inspires marketers to think creatively and adapt to changing consumer behaviors.

In conclusion, cultivating continuous learning and adaptation is non-negotiable in the marketing field. Embrace a growth mindset, stay updated with industry trends, and continuously adapt your strategies to meet the evolving needs of customers. By consistently seeking knowledge, experimenting with new approaches, and adopting an agile mindset, you can ensure your marketing efforts remain effective and relevant in an ever-changing world.

Unleashing Your Full Marketing Potential

In the ever-evolving world of marketing, achieving outstanding success requires tapping into your full marketing potential. This involves strategic planning, innovative ideas, and a strong understanding of your target audience. In this section, we will explore practical tips and strategies to help you maximize marketing effectiveness, ultimately propelling your business to new heights.

 Understanding Your Target Audience: The First Step to Success

One of the fundamental pillars of a successful marketing campaign is a deep understanding of your target audience. It is essential to delve into their habits, preferences, and needs. By gathering valuable insights about their demographics, psychographics, and behaviors, you can tailor your marketing efforts to resonate with them on a deeper level.

Consider the case of Nike, a sporting goods brand that recognized the needs and aspirations of a growing fitness-conscious demographic. By embracing a data-driven approach and analyzing consumer trends, Nike developed tailored marketing campaigns that spoke directly to their desired audience. This enabled them to connect with individuals on a personal level and created an emotional bond with their brand.

 Creating a Solid Brand Identity: The Key to Recognition and Loyalty

Building a solid brand identity is crucial for standing out in a crowded marketplace. A strong brand identity not only attracts customers but also cultivates loyalty, driving repeat business and word-of-mouth referrals. To shape your brand identity, focus on developing a unique value proposition, consistent messaging, and powerful visuals that align with your target audience's aspirations and values.

Take Apple, for example. Through their sleek and innovative products, Apple has created a brand identity that exudes simplicity, sophistication, and cutting-edge technology. By consistently delivering on these brand promises and maintaining a strong visual identity across all marketing channels, Apple has cultivated a loyal following that eagerly anticipates each product launch.

Utilizing Various Marketing Channels: A Multi-Faceted Approach

To reach your target audience effectively, it is crucial to leverage various marketing channels. Gone are the days of relying solely on traditional advertising. Today, businesses must integrate digital platforms, social media, email marketing, content marketing, and more into their marketing mix.

Dollar Shave Club revolutionized their industry with a clever video marketing campaign that quickly went viral. By utilizing YouTube, they were able to showcase their brand personality, generate buzz, and skyrocket their subscriber base. This example illustrates the vast potential of digital marketing channels and the importance of being adaptable to new platforms.

Adopting a Data-Driven Approach: Your GPS to Success

Embracing a data-driven approach is like having a GPS for your marketing campaigns. By harnessing the power of data analytics, you can gain valuable insights into customer behavior and preferences. Use these insights to inform your marketing decisions, refine your targeting, and optimize your messaging.

Gartner's CMO Spend Survey found that high-performing marketing teams allocate 15% to 20% of their budget to analytics. By investing in advanced analytics tools, these teams can track and measure the success of their campaigns, ensuring they are on the right track to achieving outstanding results.

Leveraging Social Media Platforms: The Modern Marketing Arsenal

The rise of social media platforms has opened up new opportunities for businesses to engage with their target audience. By leveraging social media, you can foster meaningful relationships, amplify brand awareness, and create viral content. Moreover, social media platforms provide valuable data and analytics to help refine your marketing strategies.

Starbucks is known for its exceptional use of social media to engage customers. Through interactive campaigns, personalized content, and influencer partnerships, Starbucks has created a highly engaged online community. By leveraging the power of user-generated content and social media influencers, Starbucks has turned their customers into brand advocates, leading to increased loyalty and advocacy.

Monitoring and Analyzing: The Path to Continuous Improvement

No marketing campaign is perfect from the start. To achieve outstanding success, it is vital to continuously monitor and analyze the performance of your marketing campaigns. By measuring key performance indicators, such as conversion rates, click-through rates, and customer acquisition costs, you can identify areas for improvement and refine your strategies accordingly.

Netflix exemplifies this commitment to improvement. By thoroughly analyzing viewer data, Netflix identifies and understands audience preferences, allowing them to personalize content recommendations and deliver the right message to the right audience. This continuous monitoring and analysis have contributed to their immense success in an increasingly competitive streaming landscape.

In conclusion, unlocking your full marketing potential requires a thoughtful combination of understanding your target audience, creating a solid brand identity, utilizing various marketing channels, adopting a data-driven approach, leveraging social media platforms, and continually monitoring and analyzing your campaigns. By implementing these strategies, you can empower your marketing efforts, achieve outstanding success, and propel your business to new heights. Remember, your potential for marketing greatness is limitless.